T0328643

Cambridge Elements ≡

Elements in International Relations
edited by
Jon C. W. Pevehouse
University of Wisconsin-Madison
Tanja A. Börzel
Freie Universität Berlin
Edward D. Mansfield
University of Pennsylvania

Associate Editors- International Security
Sarah Kreps
Cornell University
Anna Leander
Graduate Institute Geneva

TOKEN FORCES

How Tiny Troop Deployments Became Ubiquitous in UN Peacekeeping

Katharina P. Coleman
University of British Columbia
Xiaojun Li
University of British Columbia

CAMBRIDGE
UNIVERSITY PRESS

CAMBRIDGE
UNIVERSITY PRESS

Shaftesbury Road, Cambridge CB2 8EA, United Kingdom

One Liberty Plaza, 20th Floor, New York, NY 10006, USA

477 Williamstown Road, Port Melbourne, VIC 3207, Australia

314–321, 3rd Floor, Plot 3, Splendor Forum, Jasola District Centre, New Delhi – 110025, India

103 Penang Road, #05–06/07, Visioncrest Commercial, Singapore 238467

Cambridge University Press is part of Cambridge University Press & Assessment, a department of the University of Cambridge.

We share the University's mission to contribute to society through the pursuit of education, learning and research at the highest international levels of excellence.

www.cambridge.org
Information on this title: www.cambridge.org/9781009048835

DOI: 10.1017/9781009049498

First published 2022

A catalogue record for this publication is available from the British Library.

ISBN 978-1-009-04883-5 Paperback
ISSN 2515-706X (online)
ISSN 2515-7302 (print)

Token Forces

How Tiny Troop Deployments Became Ubiquitous in UN Peacekeeping

Elements in International Relations

DOI: 10.1017/9781009049498
First published online: November 2022

Katharina P. Coleman
University of British Columbia

Xiaojun Li
University of British Columbia

Author for correspondence: Katharina P. Coleman, katharina.coleman@ubc.ca

Abstract: Token forces – tiny national troop contributions in much larger coalitions – have become ubiquitous in UN peacekeeping. This Element examines how and why this contribution type has become the most common form of participation in UN peace operations despite its limited relevance for the missions' operational success. It conceptualizes token forces as a path-dependent unintended consequence of the norm of multilateralism in international uses of military force. The norm extends states' participation options by giving coalition builders an incentive to accept token forces. UN-specific types of token forces emerged as states learned about this option and secretariat officials adapted to state demand for it. The Element documents the growing incidence of token forces in UN peacekeeping, identifies the factors disposing states to contribute token forces, and discusses how UN officials channel token participation. The Element contributes to literatures on UN peacekeeping, military coalitions, and the impacts of norms in international organizations.

Keywords: peacekeeping, United Nations, norm, military coalition, legitimacy

ISBNs: 9781009048835 (PB), 9781009049498 (OC)
ISSNs: 2515-706X (online), 2515-7302 (print)

Contents

1 The Significance of Token Forces   1

2 The Ubiquity of Token Forces in UN Peace Operations   13

3 The Diffusion of Token Participation among UN Troop
  Contributors   32

4 Token Forces from the UN's Perspective   46

5 Conclusion   65

  Abbreviations   74

  Appendix   76

  References   83

1 The Significance of Token Forces

How and why did token troop contributions – tiny military deployments within much larger coalitions – become the most common form of state participation in UN peace operations? In December 2020, the UN mission in the Democratic Republic of Congo (MONUSCO) had 48 troop-contributing countries (TCCs), but 93% of its 12,758 troops were deployed by just 10 states.[1] Thirty-five MONUSCO troop contributors deployed less than 40 troops (roughly equivalent to a platoon) each, including 27 states contributing fewer than 10 troops each. Collectively, these token contributors accounted for just 200 MONUSCO troops. Likewise, 32 of the 50 TCCs in the UN mission in the Central African Republic, MINUSCA, deployed fewer than 40 troops each, jointly contributing just 168 of the mission's 11,457 military personnel. As we show in this Element, similar patterns are observable in other UN missions, consolidating from the mid-2000s onward.

Token troop contributors to UN peace operations include relatively poor states – for example, Burkina Faso contributed six MINUSCA troops in 2020 – and small states, such as Moldova (four MINUSCA troops) and Bhutan (two troops each in MONUSCO and MINUSCA). However, they also include states with far larger military capacities. Token contributors to MINUSCA include Brazil, China, France, and the USA. In MONUSCO, Sierra Leone and the USA contributed the same number of troops: three. Some states make only token troop contributions, but many combine token contributions to one mission with larger deployments in other operations (Coleman, 2013). While some token troop contributions – which we also refer to as "token forces" – grow over time, others are remarkably stable: Mongolia, for example, increased its deployment in South Sudan from 2 in 2011 to 871 in 2020, but has participated in MONUSCO (previously MONUC) with 1 or 2 troops since October 2002.

The puzzle is not only why states make token troop contributions, though to date this has been the focus of the (sparse) scholarship on the phenomenon. States cannot deploy to a UN peace operation unless the UN accepts their personnel contribution. Why does the UN welcome token forces? Multinationalism notoriously complicates military operations. As the US Joint Chiefs of Staff (2007, p. xiii) note, "The basic challenge of multinational operations is the effective integration and synchronization of available assets towards the achievement of common objectives." When coalition members deploy large numbers of troops, the military capabilities they contribute are likely to outweigh the

---

[1] Data in this paragraph are from the United Nations (2020b). We use "troop" to refer to any military personnel, including contingent members, military observers, and staff officers. We explore these distinctions later in this section and Section 3.

multinationalism costs they impose. As Winston Churchill quipped, "there is only one thing worse than fighting with allies, and that is fighting without them" (Pierre, 2002, p. 13). The peculiarity of token troop contributions, however, is that they appear to offer very limited military capabilities to offset any costs of including them in a coalition. Thus, token forces risk undermining rather than contributing to the effectiveness of UN peace operations. Why, then, have UN coalition builders welcomed them in such numbers, both in the 2000s – when the UN faced persistent troop shortages and could have accommodated larger deployments from token contributors (Passmore et al., 2018) – and since 2015, when downsizing missions with shrinking personnel needs might have allowed the UN to dispense with token contributions altogether?

We argue that the presence of token forces in UN peace operations is rooted in legitimacy rather than capability-aggregation considerations, providing important evidence for scholarly debates about the relative importance of these factors in contemporary military coalition building. However, the theoretical significance of token forces extends beyond this insight, revealing the dynamic and path-dependent interplay of global norms, states, and international organizations over time. We contend, first, that the phenomenon of token forces in UN missions illustrates that international norms can have unintended consequences: token forces emerged as an unforeseen extension of the global norm enjoining multinationalism in the international use of military force. Second, UN token forces provide insight into how states identify opportunities created by their normative environment: states learned by observation to avail themselves of, and ultimately expect, the option of token participation in UN operations. Finally, the case highlights how international organizations enmeshed in global norm dynamics also exert agency in adapting to them. To preserve peacekeeping effectiveness, UN coalition builders have sought ways to pursue both capability aggregation and legitimacy. While efforts to induce token contributors to increase their personnel commitments have had limited success, the UN has developed a system for strategically accommodating token forces that maximizes their operational benefits while mitigating adverse effects.

In this section, we present and situate our theoretical argument. We also discuss our data sources to lay the groundwork for the empirical investigation of UN token forces that follows in subsequent sections. The section ends with an overview of the remainder of the Element.

The Theoretical Significance of UN Token Forces

To date, the theoretical significance of token forces has been neglected. Where they have been recognized, these troop contributions have primarily been understood as political (and methodological) challenges to be overcome rather than complex phenomena for international relations (IR) scholars to explore.

Coleman (2013) identified token forces as a distinctive and common contribution mode, challenging the assumption that they are merely a residual category reflecting resource constraints. She also cogently identified three types of token contributions: *contingent troops* (typically deployed within another TCC's formed military unit); *military observers* (unarmed officers monitoring security and humanitarian developments in a particular area); and *staff officers*, who work within mission headquarters. Coleman offered only a cursory overview of the emergence of token forces, however, and was silent on why UN coalition builders accept token forces. She focused largely on state motivations for making token contributions, highlighting both general benefits (low-cost participation in highly legitimate operations) and specific advantages of particular token contribution types, which we return to and build on in Section 3. Coleman concluded by cautioning that token forces may undermine UN force-generation efforts – and thus threaten peacekeeping effectiveness – as states capable of deploying substantial military contingents instead choose token participation.

Token forces have since been documented in the deployment portfolios of a wide range of states (Gjevori & Visoka, 2018; Solar, 2019; Young, 2019). Yet most analytical attention has focused on overcoming tokenism, reflecting awareness that peacekeeping effectiveness depends heavily on the number of deployed peacekeepers (Hultman et al., 2013) as well as the quality (Haass & Ansorg, 2018) and diversity (Bove et al., 2020) of large military contingents. Thus, studies have highlighted states moving from token to non-token contributions (e.g., Kenkel et al., 2020), investigated the efficacy of economic incentives to increase troop contributions (Henke, 2019; Boutton & D'Orazio, 2020), and assessed the potential for Western states to reemerge as substantial rather than token troop contributors (Raitasalo, 2014; Koops & Tercovich, 2016). Scholars have also increasingly addressed the methodological risk of token forces skewing quantitative analyses of the motivations of (major) TCCs (Coleman & Nyblade, 2018; Duursma & Gledhill, 2019), including by distinguishing between participation and contribution size (Kathman & Melin, 2017), excluding token contributions (Lundgren et al., 2021), or ascertaining the impact of token forces in robustness checks (Ward & Dorussen, 2016). Beyond providing greater confidence in results, doing so may reveal the full power of a causal mechanism.[2]

---

[2] Henke (2019) finds that excluding token forces reveals an increased substantive effect of diplomatic embeddedness in coalition building.

While generating significant insights, this "problem-solving" approach has left important empirical and theoretical questions about token forces as a distinctive, common, and stable contribution mode underexplored. Empirically, we lack systematic data about the evolution of token forces in UN operations, changes in the number and identity of token contributors over time, and the patterns of tokenism across missions. We address these gaps in subsequent sections. Here, we focus on the core theoretical question of how and why tokenism has expanded so dramatically in UN peacekeeping over the past three decades. Our answer contributes to a long-standing debate about the relative weight of capability aggregation and legitimacy considerations in contemporary coalition building by situating it within the dynamic interplay of global norms, states, and international organizations.

UN Peace Operations as Coalitions

Scholars of military coalitions often ignore UN missions, but there is no cogent reason for doing so. Weitsman, who influentially defined military coalitions as "ad hoc multinational understandings that are forged to undertake a specific mission, and . . . dissolve once that mission is complete," explicitly distinguished them from "multilateral effort[s] organized and sanctioned by global international institutions such as the [UN]" (2013, pp. 35–6, 25). However, the presence of an institutional framework cannot serve to differentiate UN missions from coalition operations. Operations by NATO are routinely studied as coalitions (Kreps, 2011). Many ad hoc coalitions have UN mandates.[3] Most importantly, UN peacekeeping forces are also forged for particular operations and disbanded when a mission ends. The UN has no standing army, and participation in UN missions is voluntary: states make case-by-case decisions about whether to deploy personnel to a particular operation. Thus, as one former UN official noted, "every mission becomes a coalition of the willing" (UN_HQ14).[4] Moreover, UN operations have increasingly been deployed in ongoing conflicts and mandated to engage in offensive military operations (Karlsrud, 2015), so "the lines that once clearly delineated UN operations from other types of multilateral interventions are today very fuzzy indeed" (Henke, 2019, p. 171). United Nations peacekeeping coalitions do exhibit some distinctive features, including the high incidence of token forces we explore in this Element. Yet none of these particularities obviates the fact that UN missions feature military coalitions.

---

[3] Examples include the 1991 Gulf War coalition, the 1999 International Force East Timor, and the 2013 African-led International Support Mission in Mali.

[4] See upcoming subsection "UN Token Forces: Norms, States, and IOs Interacting Over Time"on referencing interviews.

United Nations bureaucrats play a central role in building these coalitions. They do not work in isolation: powerful states with national interests in particular UN operations are often pivotal in inducing other states to join peacekeeping coalitions (Henke, 2019), and state-led peacekeeping summits and ministerial meetings are important in mobilizing contribution pledges. Ultimately, however, states can only deploy into a UN operation if the UN – specifically, the Under-Secretary-General for Peace Operations – formally invites their contribution. For each mission, the Office of Military Affairs (OMA) within the Department of Peace Operations (DPO) develops and updates a Concept of Operations, a Statement of Force Requirements (SFR) specifying the number and type of military units needed, and Statements of Unit Requirements detailing the composition, equipment, and tasks of each unit (UN, 2021h, p. 22). Officials from OMA solicit state participation and assess the degree to which proposed contributions meet mission requirements, a task facilitated since 2015 by the Peacekeeping Capabilities Readiness System (PCRS), which allows for longer-term UN engagement with potential troop contributors (Coleman et al., 2021). Assessments by OMA are not the sole factor determining which proposed contributions are accepted: the UN's ability to be selective depends on the availability of alternative troop contributions and, as we show in Section 3, decisions on proposed contributions also respond to political pressures, including the deployment expectations of member states. Nevertheless, UN officials exercise final authority to accept or decline troop contributions and thus act as key coalition architects.

UN Token Forces as a Puzzle: Capability Aggregation and Legitimacy in Coalition Building

Contemporary military coalitions have long been recognized as serving two broad functions: "Militarily, they distribute the task and the responsibilities; politically, they help provide the legitimacy that is needed in the eyes of the world community for military action" (Pierre, 2002, p. 1). Each function provides a distinct rationale for coalition building. The capability-aggregation rationale holds that states build coalitions to pool military assets and effort, which enables them to undertake operations they are unable or unwilling to execute alone. The legitimacy rationale suggests intervenors build coalitions to establish benign intent: "Multilateralism legitimizes action by signalling broad support for the actor's goals. Intervenors use it to demonstrate that their purpose is not merely self-serving and particularistic but is joined in some way to community interests that other states share" (Finnemore, 2003, p. 82).

There has been extensive debate over the relative importance of these two rationales in contemporary coalition building. Capability-aggregation dominated (neo)realist accounts of Cold War alliances as institutions for power balancing (Waltz, 1979; Walt, 1987), whose "primary function [was] to pool military strength against a common enemy" (Snyder, 1997), despite potentially suboptimal burden sharing (Olson & Zeckhauser, 1966). After the Cold War, some scholars cautioned that coalition builders were allowing the legitimacy rationale to crowd out capability-aggregation considerations, seeking broad, unwieldy coalitions "for the purpose of representing international support and legitimacy for an action . . . [that] may detract from actual war-fighting capability" (Weitsman, 2013, p. 25).[5] Yet multiple studies have disputed this claim, arguing that coalition size and structure still largely reflect coalition builders' expectations about the operational commitment an intervention will entail, and thus a capability-aggregation rationale (Kreps, 2011; Wolford, 2015). Coalition builders accept the efficiency costs of coalitions because they are balanced by burden sharing and overall capability gains (Recchia, 2015; Morey, 2016). Legitimacy considerations shape whether coalition builders seek an international mandate for intervention, but have limited effect on coalition structure (Kreps, 2011; Johns & Davies, 2014; Schmitt, 2019).

However, the abundance of token forces in UN missions is difficult to explain from a capability-aggregation perspective. Small troop contributions often provide limited capabilities whose marginal impact on peacekeeping effectiveness may not outweigh the efficiency costs of adding them to the coalition:

> [S]ending only a handful of soldiers to an operation can actually be harmful for the totality. . . . Managing a troop matrix of dozens of small contributions means a lot of extra administrative work, not to mention the added negative side effects of trying to assimilate multiple military and national cultures into a functioning entity. (Raitasalo, 2014, p. 379)[6]

There are exceptions: "small contributions can be very significant, particularly when they are deployed in niche areas. For example, give me a very well-trained, pre-formed thirty-person human intelligence gathering team and you can generate some very impressive effects with that" (ISAF_22). Yet niche capabilities are defined by their scarcity, both within national militaries and within missions, while token forces are the most common mode of state participation in UN peacekeeping, as noted earlier and demonstrated in Section 2. The question from a capability-aggregation perspective is what kinds of (niche) capabilities all these token forces provide that are not readily available from larger coalition members.

---

5 See also Bensahel (2007, p. 201) and Finnemore (2003, p. 82).
6 See also Schmitt (2019, p. 74).

It is tempting to conclude that the ubiquity of token forces in UN missions signals the ascendance of the legitimacy rationale in UN coalition building. As we explore further in Section 4, UN officials are certainly sensitive to the legitimacy benefits of a large coalition: "you want a force that represents the whole world as much as possible, so it's the power of symbolism, it's the trust, it's the notion that the UN is not aligned behind a particular agenda" (UN_HQ2). However, a legitimacy-based explanation for UN token forces raises two questions.

First, why is tokenism so prevalent in UN operations? These missions are authorized by the Security Council, establishing both their legality and their international legitimacy (Finnemore, 2003, p. 81; Voeten, 2005; Thompson, 2006; Coleman, 2007). They are also relatively insulated from charges of masking major-power incursions in host countries. There are cogent critiques of Western domination of UN mandating decisions (e.g., Cunliffe, 2013). However, since the mid-1990s, Western states have rarely deployed major UN peacekeeping contingents and have tended to address crises in which they perceived major national interests through NATO or ad hoc coalitions, where possible with a UN mandate. They are thus more plausibly charged with using UN peacekeeping to avoid addressing crises they consider of marginal strategic interest more directly than with launching self-interested military interventions under the UN flag: "UN missions [are] for global public benefits and non-UN missions for peacekeeper-specific benefits" (Gaibulloev et al., 2009, p. 827). If so, UN operations should have relatively little need for legitimation.

Second, why would UN coalition builders turn specifically to token forces as sources of additional legitimacy for UN operations? UN peacekeeping expanded rapidly in 2000–15 and faced persistent personnel shortages (HIPPO, 2015, pp. 9–11; Passmore et al., 2018). United Nations coalition builders therefore had reason to eschew token troop contributions in favor of substantial ones offering both greater military capabilities and the legitimating effect of an additional troop contributor. Moreover, substantial contributions may present two legitimacy advantages over token ones. In bolstering a mission's capabilities, they can help increase peacekeeping effectiveness, strengthening "outcome legitimacy" (Finnemore, 2005; Hurrell, 2005, pp. 22–3). As the UN recognizes, "[a] mission's legitimacy and credibility rely on the consistency of its support to the human rights agenda and its ability to meet protection expectations" (UN, 2020a, p. 27). Substantial troop commitments may also signal greater political support of the operation by the troop contributors and thus a more credible multinationalism:

> a country which made the clear and conscious political choice to be heavily integrated with the leading state is making a political statement which has a much more important impact on the legitimacy of the operation than any token contribution, as numerous as they may be. (Schmitt, 2019, p. 77)

Thus, neither capability aggregation nor legitimacy considerations fully explain the ubiquity of token forces in UN peacekeeping coalitions. The problem, we maintain, lies with framing these two rationales as dichotomous options in a static conception of coalition builder choice. We propose recasting them as elements of an interactive dynamic between international norms, coalition builders, and (potential) troop contributors that evolves over time.

UN Token Forces: Norms, States, and IOs Interacting Over Time

The legitimacy rationale cogently highlights that a troop contribution can be valuable to coalition builders even if it does not add significantly to overall mission capabilities. This value arises from the contemporary global norm that international uses of military force should be multinational to certify that they serve international rather than purely national ends (Coleman, 2007, pp. 44–5). In this sense, the global norm of multinationalism in international uses of military force is at the root of the phenomenon of token forces, including in UN operations.[7]

However, the global military multinationalism norm is at best silent about token forces, enjoining intervenors to build coalitions but not specifying contribution size. As noted, it may even favor substantial troop contributions (signaling more genuine multinationalism) over token ones. The norm also specifies appropriate behavior only for coalition builders; there is no general global norm enjoining token participation in military coalitions. Consequently, token forces are best understood as an *unintended consequence* of the contemporary military multinationalism norm.

This conceptualization builds on the historical institutionalist scholarship of Comparative Politics, which has long stressed that social and political institutions can have important unexpected consequences that emerge over time (Pierson & Skocpol, 2002). Unintended consequences often arise through conflicts among a polity's various institutions (March & Olsen, 1983, p. 743; Hall & Taylor, 1996, p. 942; Thelen, 1999, p. 382), but they are also driven by strategic actors who perceive and exploit opportunities to redirect institutions for originally unintended ends. Redirection may reflect dominant actors' shifting priorities or changing power relations among social groups seeking different ends (Cortell & Peterson, 2001, pp. 775–6; Thelen, 2004, p. 36). It may also

---

[7] We touch on tokenism in non-UN operations in Sections 4 and 5.

occur because an evolving constellation of institutions provides "unintended openings for actors" to pursue their interests in novel ways (Pierson & Skocpol, 2002, p. 706). Such strategic actions can undermine an institution's original goal (Cortell & Peterson, 2001; Thelen, 2004, p. 36; Paul, 2008) but need not have deleterious effects: "undesired effects are not always undesirable effects" (Merton, 1936, p. 895). Importantly, strategic behavior can diffuse within a polity over time. Actors are "knowledgeable and reflective" agents who do not have complete information about the range of "feasible, possible and indeed desirable" behaviors in their institutional context but learn by monitoring the consequences of both their own actions and others' strategic behaviors (Hay & Wincott, 1998, pp. 955–6). Thus, strategic action by one agent can produce a broader phenomenon of unintended behavior as all actors learn what the institutional context will allow.

International Relations scholars have explored unintended consequences of norm advocacy (Weeks, 2017; Bradley, 2019; Snyder, 2020) and other normatively inscribed international activities, including peacekeeping (e.g., Jennings, 2010; von Billerbeck & Tansey, 2019), but have tended to focus on unforeseen implementation effects rather than unintended consequences arising from the existence of norms themselves. Yet international norms are recognized as enabling as well as constraining behavior (Wheeler, 2000; Hurd, 2017). A historical institutionalist perspective adds that international norms may unintentionally enable a different behavior from the one they were created to promote, either instead of or in addition to the original target behavior.

Token forces can arise through strategic behavior by coalition builders. The 2003 US-led intervention in Iraq, for example, raised charges of "anemic" multilateralism (or "unilateralism masquerading as multilateralism"), where the coalition builder recruits token contributors to legitimize an intervention it dominates operationally and strategically (Kreps, 2011, p. 17). As noted, however, UN coalition builders have little incentive to strategically recruit token forces because UN operations already enjoy substantial international legitimacy. In the UN case, therefore, strategic behavior is more plausibly attributed to token troop contributors. As we explore further in Section 3, states that are unwilling or unable to deploy a substantial number of troops to a UN mission may prefer token to nonparticipation, given the political rewards of (low-cost) participation in legitimate operations and the possibility of gaining operational influence (through staff officers), information (through military observers), and/or training benefits (from co-deployed contingent troops) (Coleman, 2013; Rahbek-Clemmensen, 2019). These states do not seek to circumvent the intended effect of the military multinationalism norm (curbing self-interested military interventions) but to take advantage of the opportunity the norm unintentionally creates by giving UN coalition builders a reason to accept token forces even if they do not enhance overall coalition capability. As more states learn about this opportunity over time, including by observing others' token contributions to UN missions, the demand for token participation increases. Once they understand that token forces are a viable participation mode in UN operations, states will seek this opportunity whenever they judge it preferable to both substantial and nonparticipation in a mission.

UN coalition builders face a different – but also dynamic – strategic calculation. The starting point, as noted, is: (1) the global military multinationalism norm provides a reason to accept token contributions, but (2) the relatively high legitimacy of UN missions limits coalition builders' demand for token forces, and (3) unless a mission already has all its required capabilities, substantial troop contributions are likely to be preferable to token ones because they provide equal (or greater) legitimacy benefits while also serving capability-aggregation goals. As we elaborate further in Section 4, three dynamics extend from this starting point.

First, when missions face capability gaps, UN coalition builders' willingness to accept token forces is inversely related to their ability to induce states to make larger troop commitments that fill those gaps. As historical institutionalists note, unintended consequences often reflect the balance of power among a polity's actors (Cortell & Peterson, 2001, pp. 768–99; Thelen, 2004, p. 36). Tokenism in understaffed missions reflects the power balance between states preferring token to substantial participation and UN coalition builders with both legitimacy and capability-aggregation aims. While the UN's capacity to elicit more substantial contributions is likely to vary by troop contributor and by mission, the high incidence of tokenism in UN operations – especially from states capable of larger deployments – suggests the UN is generally weak in this regard.

Second, an escalating demand for token participation in UN missions reverberates in the strategic calculations of UN coalition builders. As states learn about the opportunity to participate in UN missions with token forces through their own experience and/or by observing others, they update their expectations that an offer of token forces will be accepted. As such expectations rise, the political costs to the UN of refusing them increase. Over time, an institutional norm – a UN-specific standard of expected behavior – may emerge that UN coalition builders should generally accept token contributions, allowing states to participate in UN peacekeeping in this manner unless there are strong countervailing reasons. Acceptance of token forces becomes the default position and rejection requires justification. In this altered normative environment, accepting token forces acquires new legitimacy advantages, where the legitimacy audience is UN member states themselves. States' support for an operation – and UN peacekeeping in general – may increase when they are able to participate with token forces but wane otherwise.

Third, UN coalition builders facing increasing pressure to accept token forces will seek to channel these contributions in ways that maximize their operational benefits or at least minimize negative impacts on operational capacity, thus serving or at least preserving peacekeeping effectiveness. Capability-aggregation concerns are not eclipsed by the normative and strategic shift toward accepting token forces but must be adapted to this new reality. As noted, token contributions to UN operations take three principal forms: staff officers, military observers, and co-deployed contingent troops. United Nations coalition builders are limited in their ability to refuse token forces or induce states to increase their troop commitments, but they can shape the kinds of token contributions they accept. Depending on mission circumstances, they may eschew token contribution types that are particularly detrimental to operational effectiveness, in favor of those presenting less risk of aggregate capability losses. They can also restrict particularly desirable types of token contributions to the most powerful contributors and/or those providing especially high-quality troops. Over time, states will learn of these adaptations and may update their expectations about the tokenism options available to them.

In short, the global military multinationalism norm does not simply produce a static shift in the relative weight of capability aggregation and legitimacy in UN coalition building. Instead, the changed normative environment alters the strategic behavior of both coalition builders and potential coalition members, each learning over time about the new opportunities they are afforded and the constraints they face, and adjusting their expectations and strategies accordingly. These adjustments, in turn, have repercussions for other members of the polity, who adjust again until eventually a new equilibrium set of expectations and behaviors is reached.

There is no reason to expect these general processes to be unique to the UN. The global military multinationalism norm has altered the normative environment for all actors engaged in peace operations, including NATO, regional organizations, and ad hoc coalitions of the willing. The nature of the impact, however, will be mediated by a number of factors, including states' demand for token over nonparticipation, coalition builders' capacity to pressure would-be contributors to enhance their troop commitments, and differing strategies for accommodating token forces operationally. Each of these will likely have its own repercussions, leading to distinctive path-dependent developments in each institutional context. In this Element, we focus primarily on the UN context, though we offer a comparison to NATO in Section 4. We suggest in our Conclusion that more comprehensive comparative work is warranted.

Data Sources and the UN Token Forces Dataset

We use quantitative and qualitative methods to investigate the phenomenon of token forces in UN peace operations. For our quantitative analyses, we constructed the *UN Token Forces Dataset* (UNTFD) as detailed in Section 2. The UNTFD draws on the International Peace Institute (IPI) Peacekeeping Database (Perry & Smith, 2013), which records uniformed personnel contributions to post-Cold War UN peace operations by TCCs, month, peacekeeper type, and mission. For reasons discussed in Section 2, we set aside the police data and focus on military personnel contributions, noting that the data allow us to distinguish military observers (also identified as "experts on mission") as one potential type of token troop contribution but conflate the other two types: UN data only began distinguishing staff officers from contingent troops in December 2017. Measuring the deployment of token forces and other modes of contributions at different levels of aggregation (country, mission, and year), the UNTFD enables us to uncover the evolution of token forces over time in Section 2. In Section 3, we merge the UNTFD with other existing datasets in IR to facilitate our inquiries on the diffusion of token contributions among TCCs.

Our qualitative evidence includes 145 interviews conducted between 2008 and 2021 about token forces in UN and other coalition operations. This includes 22 interviews with current or former officials at UN Headquarters in New York; 18 interviews with civilian and military peacekeepers in the UN mission in Cyprus (UNFICYP) in 2010; and 47 interviews with current or former MONUSCO peacekeepers, of which 41 occurred during a 2017 research visit. Fifty-six interviews, predominantly in 2010–11 with military and civilian personnel at NATO Headquarters (Brussels, Belgium), NATO Military Headquarters (Mons, Belgium), and US Central Command (Tampa, USA), focused on NATO's International Security Assistance Force (ISAF) in Afghanistan, though many also included discussion of the 2003 USA-led intervention in Iraq (MNF-I). The final two interviews, conducted in the United Kingdom in 2011, focused on MNF-I only. To preserve anonymity, these interviews have been anonymized and randomly assigned numbers within four ranges: UN_HQ1 to UN_HQ22 for UN Headquarters officials; UN_PK1 to UN_PK65 for UN peacekeepers, with * appended for civilian and top military officials directly representing the UN; ISAF_1 to ISAF_56 for ISAF-related interviews; and Iraq_1 and Iraq_2 for the remaining two interviews.

Overview of Remaining Sections

Section 2 highlights the emergence of token forces as the dominant mode of state participation in UN peacekeeping. It begins by noting the paucity of token forces in Cold War UN peacekeeping and their tentative emergence by the early 1990s. The section then introduces the UNTFD and proceeds to use these data to establish that token forces have become common in UN peacekeeping overall, ubiquitous across missions, persistent over mission life spans, and widespread among peacekeeping contributors.

Section 3 focuses on the motivations of token troop contributors and the diffusion of token participation among states. It begins by identifying the factors that may lead states to prefer token participation in a UN mission to either substantial deployment or nonparticipation. To act on this preference, however, states must recognize it as a viable participation option in UN missions. Drawing on the diffusion literature in IR, this section conceptualizes a learning process over time in which states discern the viability of token participation in part by observing other states' deployments. It then presents empirical support for this argument, demonstrating a strong and robust learning effect on contribution choice, in addition to common explanations based on resource constraints, international interests, and domestic political systems.

Section 4 considers token forces from the UN's perspective and asks why UN coalition builders accept the deployment of token forces. It highlights four key factors. First, UN coalition builders recognize the international legitimacy benefits of broad coalitions, though they typically do not perceive major legitimacy challenges for UN missions. Second, the UN has limited capacity to persuade token troop contributors to increase their deployments, a fact underlined by comparison with NATO's ISAF operation. Third, UN coalition builders are both normatively committed to inclusiveness in peacekeeping and pragmatically motivated to keep states – including powerful states – invested in UN peacekeeping. Finally, the three distinct mechanisms (co-deployed contingent personnel, staff officer deployments, and military observer positions) UN missions have evolved to accommodate token participation demands have path-dependent effects, as UN coalition builders now routinely – though selectively – mobilize these mechanisms to welcome token forces.

Section 5 summarizes the main findings, discusses their theoretical and policy implications, and identifies directions for future research.

2 The Ubiquity of Token Forces in UN Peace Operations

For most of the Cold War, token forces were discouraged in UN peacekeeping. The Force Commander of the UN's first peacekeeping force,

UNEF (1956–67), favored "contingents of not less than battalion strength, believing that a force of small units of different nationalities would be difficult to control" (Wainhouse, 1973, p. 222). Secretary-General Dag Hammarskjold agreed:

> it is desirable that countries participating in the Force should provide self-contained units in order to avoid the loss of time and efficiency which is unavoidable when new units are set up through joining together small groups of different nationalities. (UN Secretary-General, 1956, p. 6)

Consequently, although a total of 24 countries offered troops, UNEF's initial military coalition included only 10 states, and the smallest national contingent among them numbered 255 troops.

The 1960–64 operation in the Congo (ONUC) departed from this force structure, not least for legitimacy considerations: Hammarskjold "wanted to assuage the concerns of the then newly emerging Afro-Asian group that the UN was not simply about replacing the former colonial masters with a new set of neocolonialists" (UN_PK66*). The broad coalition for ONUC included staff officers from Ceylon (Sri Lanka), New Zealand, and Burma, and small specialist units from Argentina, Austria, Brazil, Iran, the Netherlands, the Philippines, and Yugoslavia (UN, 1960, Annex 1; Wainhouse, 1973, pp. 305–30). However, ONUC proved a controversial, costly operation that neither UN officials nor member states sought to replicate. The UN Peacekeeping Force in Cyprus (UNFICYP), established in 1964, mirrored UNEF in deploying large, operationally autonomous units (Wainhouse, 1973, p. 356): Canada, Denmark, Finland, Ireland, Sweden, and the United Kingdom contributed between 799 and 1,132 troops each (UN Secretary-General, 1964). The only outlier was Austria, whose offer of a field hospital (47 personnel) was accepted reluctantly. Austria faced considerable pressure to augment its contribution and increased its commitment to 336 troops in 1972. The UN Disengagement Observer Force in the Golan Heights, mandated in 1974, included substantial contingents from Austria, Canada, Peru, and Poland, with six headquarters staff seconded from UNEF and 89 military observers detailed from the UN Truce Supervision Organization in the Middle East (UNTSO), without attribution to any TCC (UN Secretary-General, 1975, p. 2). The UN Interim Force in Lebanon (UNIFIL, created 1978) similarly deployed with substantial contributions from eight TCCs and was "assisted" by 37 UNTSO military observers (UN Secretary-General, 1979, p. 2).

Precedents for token forces emerged along distinctive pathways. For token staff officer contributions, UNFICYP set an early precedent: from the 1970s onward, substantial UNFICYP troop contributors that ceased deploying formed units nevertheless retained staff officer positions. Ireland transitioned to token staff officer contributions in 1973, Finland in 1976, Sweden in 1987, Denmark in 1993, Canada in 1994, and Austria in 2002.[8] These token contributions proved persistent – Canada and Austria still maintain theirs, though Austria's eventual ceding of the Chief Operations Officer post to Argentina also foreshadowed how major TCCs can challenge token contributors' incumbency of key staff officer positions (UN_PK33).

Token military observer (UNMO) contributions became a significant participation option as post-Cold War missions formally included both military observers and formed military units in their force structure. At various times UNPROFOR in the former Yugoslavia (1992–5) received token contributions including UNMOs from Australia, Brazil, Ghana, India, Ireland, Lithuania, Switzerland, and Venezuela. Token UNMO contributions became more fully established when two operations that began as observer missions – MONUC in the Democratic Republic of Congo (1999–2010) and UNMEE between Ethiopia and Eritrea (2000–08) – expanded to also include a more substantial military presence. Of the 201 yearly token contributions observed in MONUC, 80% included UNMOs, and 66% included only UNMOs. In UNMEE, 92% of yearly token contributions included UNMOs, and 66% included only UNMOs.

For token contingent personnel contributions, UNFICYP was again precedent setting. Argentina became a major UNFICYP troop contributor in 1993, assuming responsibility for the mission's Sector 1. In 1995, Brazil deployed two troops into the sector and in exchange allowed Argentina to fill two Brazilian positions in the UN mission in Angola (De Andrade, 2001, p. 10). By 1999, Argentina's UNFICYP contingent included troops from Bolivia (two), Brazil (two), Paraguay (one), and Uruguay (three) (UN Secretary-General, 1999). Argentina subsequently registered Bolivia, Brazil, Chile, Paraguay, Peru, and Uruguay with the UN as potential troop contributors to its Sector 1 contingent (UN_PK33). In UNFICYP's Sector 4, meanwhile, small Hungarian and Slovenian contingents deployed alongside the established Austrian contingent in 1995 and 1997, respectively.[9]

From these sporadic beginnings, token forces have developed into the most popular mode of participation in UN peacekeeping. In the rest of this section, we provide the first systematic empirical demonstration of their emergence and current ubiquity, drawing on an original dataset constructed for this purpose.

Constructing the UN Token Forces Dataset

To construct the UNTFD, we start with the IPI Peacekeeping Database, which uses UN archival records to capture states' personnel contributions to UN

---

[8] Data from UN Secretary-General mission reports.
[9] Hungary had already contributed four military observers to UNFICYP in 1993–1994.

missions in the post-Cold War period (Perry & Smith, 2013). The database records uniformed personnel contributions from each country by month, type (troop, police, or expert/observer), and mission. At the time of writing, the IPI database covers personnel contributions from 156 states to 82 peace operations and related missions over the 29-year period from November 1990 to October 2018.

We focus on military personnel contributions, which include troops and military experts/observers. We exclude police from our analysis as a different and incommensurable contribution type. The UN deploys far fewer police than military personnel (7,553 and 68,708, respectively, in July 2021) (UN, 2021b) and missions' police and military components typically perform distinct tasks. Thus, rather than attempting to specify what level of police deployment would turn a token troop contribution into a non-token overall contribution, we bracket police contributions as operationally important but separate from troop contributions. A state is classified as making a token or non-token troop contribution based on its military deployment to a mission, regardless of whether it also makes a (token or non-token) contribution to the mission's police component.

We define a TCC as making a token troop contribution if it deploys fewer than 40 troops *and* fewer than 10 military observers to a mission. This is a stringent definition. We eschew the company-level demarcation privileged by Duursma and Gledhill (2019, p. 1167) and Henke (2019, p. 49), given that deploying 100–150 troops may represent a significant effort by the TCC even if it is operationally marginal in a large mission. Instead, we use the 40-troop threshold proposed by Coleman (2013) and adopted by Koops and Tercovich (2016, p. 600) and Boutton and D'Orazio (2020, p. 319). This is roughly equivalent to one platoon, the smallest military unit UN doctrine considers capable – at least temporarily – of independent operations (UNDPKO & UNDFS, 2012, p. 52; UN_HQ5). We add the restriction on military observers because given the nature of these posts and their relative scarcity – in July 2021, UN peace operations included 1,186 UNMOs, compared to 67,522 troops and staff officers (UN, 2021b) – deploying 39 UNMOs to a mission is arguably a substantial contribution. The conservative threshold of 10 military observers more reliably limits the token designation to contributions that are both numerically insignificant within contemporary UN missions and relatively minor in terms of the TCC's deployment effort.

We removed from our dataset all missions with fewer than 1,000 troops averaged across the duration of the mission, and for missions averaging more than 1,000 troops, we removed years in which their troop deployment dropped below 1,000. We thus exclude special political missions (such as UNAMA in

Afghanistan) and observer missions (such as the UN Military Observer Group in India and Pakistan) that differ qualitatively from contemporary peacekeeping operations. The notion of token contributions also becomes less applicable, since in very small missions, even a troop contribution of fewer than 40 may be relatively significant. In all, 28 of the 47 missions we exclude in the IPI database average fewer than 10 troops for the duration of the mission, and another 9 averaged between 10 and 100 troops. A few larger missions warrant closer examination. The closest to the 1,000-troop threshold is UNPREDEP in Macedonia, with an average of 965 troops. We removed this mission, as it is to date the UN's only preventative deployment. MONUA, in Angola, averaged 849 troops over its two and a half-year lifespan. However, it deployed some 2,500 troops in its first six months before shrinking to 782 troops in 1998 and 213 in 1999. Thus, although the average deployment for the duration of the mission dips below 1,000, we retained MONUA in the dataset for the first year of its operation in 1997.

Removing the smaller missions reduces the number of missions from 82 to 35 (see Table A1 in the Appendix). The number of TCCs falls only slightly, from 156 to 151. Figure 1 plots the number of active missions with over 1,000 troops per year and the average number of troops for these missions from 1990 to 2018. The total number of active missions has broadly increased over time, but with substantial fluctuations. The decline in the late 1990s reflects the contraction of UN peacekeeping after failures in Bosnia and Herzegovina and in Somalia; the current decline arises from the closure of missions in Liberia, Sierra Leone, Côte d'Ivoire, and Haiti and the Security Council's failure to mandate any substantial new missions since 2014 (Coleman, 2020a). The average number of troops per mission mirrors the dramatic contraction of active missions in the 1990s, but in 2016–18 decreases in active missions are accompanied by increases in average troop deployments in the remaining missions. Our dataset

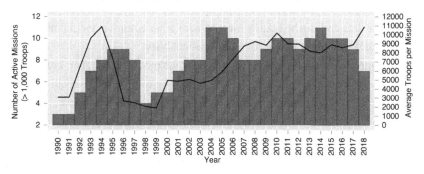

Figure 1 UN missions and troops over time
Note: The bars represent missions (left axis) and the line represents troops (right axis).
Source: UNTFD.

includes three missions active for the entire 29-year period, but since UNDOF and UNFICYP troop deployments drop below 1,000 for some years, UNIFIL is the only mission appearing in our dataset every year.

Figure 2 shows the geographical distribution of the 35 missions and 151 TCCs in the UNTFD. The vast majority of missions occurred in Africa. The exceptions are in Cambodia, East Timor, the Golan Heights, Haiti, Lebanon, and the former Yugoslavia. Of the 36 host countries, 13 had one UN mission and six had two. Sudan and the former Yugoslavia hosted three UN operations, and Haiti hosted four.

In terms of the TCCs (Figure 3), on average, they participated (i.e., made at least one, but typically multiple, yearly troop contributions) in 11.5 of the 35 missions. At the low end, 17 TCCs contributed to only one mission and 15 contributed to two. At the high end, three countries contributed to 30 or more missions: Nepal (30), Nigeria (31), and Bangladesh (31). All five permanent UN Security Council members were frequent contributors by this measure: China, France, Russia, the United Kingdom, and the USA contributed to 19, 26, 25, 21, and 23 missions, respectively. This stands in notable tension to the fact that since the early 1990s, only China has been a major UN TCC: in July 2021, China ranked 10th among 120 UN personnel contributors, with 2,249 peace-keepers deployed, France ranked 35th (608), the United Kingdom 37th (532), Russia 64th (74), and the USA 79th (32) (UN, 2021b).

Applying our token forces criteria, we generate a binary indicator of monthly tokenism for each TCC's contribution to a given mission. Out of the 121,807 country-mission-month observations in the dataset, 60,290 (49.5%) are identified as token troop contributions. Because most countries deploy their troops for at least six months, and many for a whole year, 91% of these monthly indicators do not change in a calendar year. Consequently, we can aggregate the monthly indicators for each country to annual ones without much loss of information. The aggregated annual measures help improve the interpretation and visualization of the data and can be readily merged with other common annual measures such as GDP and regime type for additional analysis.

The aggregation is performed by averaging the monthly tokenism indicators in a calendar year. This produces 8,898 country-mission-year observations. Of these, 1,657 (19%) are contributions listed in the original IPI dataset that are neither token nor non-token by our definition, notably arising from countries contributing police officers to a mission without sending any military personnel. For reasons noted earlier, we remove this category in all the analyses in this Element and focus only on troop contributions.

The remaining 7,241 tokenism measures at the country-mission-year level range from zero, meaning a TCC never contributed fewer than 40 troops or 10

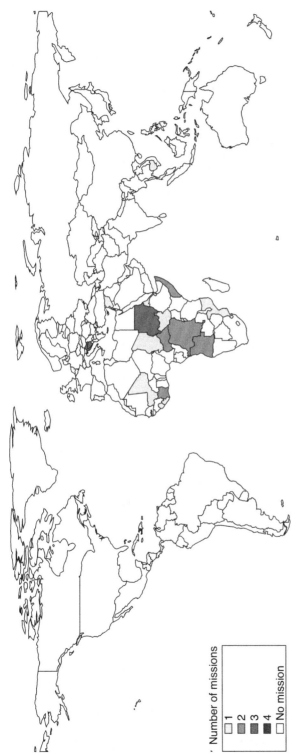

Figure 2 Locations of missions

Number of missions
1
2
3
4
No mission

Source: UNTFD.

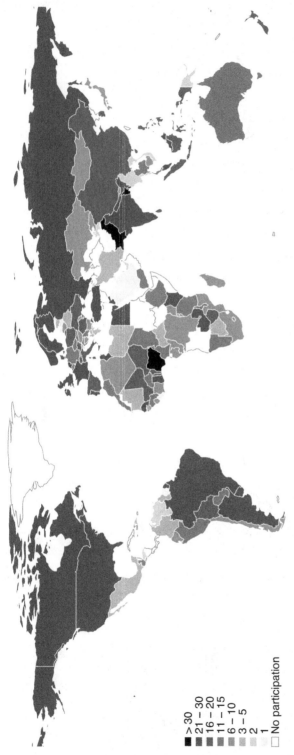

Figure 3 Participation in UN missions by TCC

> 30
21 – 30
16 – 20
11 – 15
6 – 10
3 – 5
2
1
No participation

Source: UNTFD.

military observers (or both) to a mission in a given year, to one, meaning the TCC made only token troop contributions to a mission in a given year. Values between zero and one indicate a TCC shifted from a token to a non-token troop contribution, or vice versa, for a mission during the year. This often occurs when countries join or exit a mission. For example, Argentina joined MINUSTAH with 1 troop in May 2004, deployed 6 troops the next month, 204 in July, 488 in August, and over 500 for the rest of the year. Conversely, when MINUSTAH drew down in 2017, Argentina reduced its deployment gradually, from 72 troops in January to six in September.

In what follows, we use these measures as well as their further aggregation at the mission and country levels to explore the trends and evolutions of token force contributions in UN peacekeeping operations.

Overall Pattern of Token Forces

Token forces are the most common mode of troop contribution to UN peace-keeping missions, accounting for 3,899 of the 7,241 observations (about 54%) at the country-mission-year level in the 35 missions between 1990 and 2018. They are followed by non-token troop contributions (2,604 or 36%) and mixed contributions (738 or 10%), in which a TCC switches between token and non-token contributions over the course of a year.

Token forces have become an increasingly popular mode of participation in UN missions over time. Figure 4 tracks token, mixed, and non-token troop contributions over time, both in the aggregate and as a share of total contributions.[10] It shows that token troop contributions have become increasingly common by both measures. In 1990 and 1991, when there were three active large missions, only 15% of troop contributions were token.[11] In 1992–5, as UN peacekeeping expanded (see Figure 1) and the number of active missions rose to seven, both the number and the share of token troop contributions steadily increased, and mixed contributions also emerged. The subsequent crisis in UN peacekeeping reduced the number of active large missions to a nadir of four in 1998 and produced dramatic drops in all three modes of troop contribution; the shares of token and non-token troop contributions reverted to levels observed in 1990–1.

During the resurgence of UN peacekeeping between 1999 and 2005, the number of active missions jumped from 5 to 11. Troop contributions surged at an even faster rate as more countries – notably from Asia and Africa – began to

---

[10] Since TCCs often contribute to more than one mission simultaneously, the aggregate number of troop contributions in Figure 4 exceeds the number of unique TCCs each year.

[11] Consistent with the above account of the emergence of tokenism, all these token forces were deployed in UNFICYP.

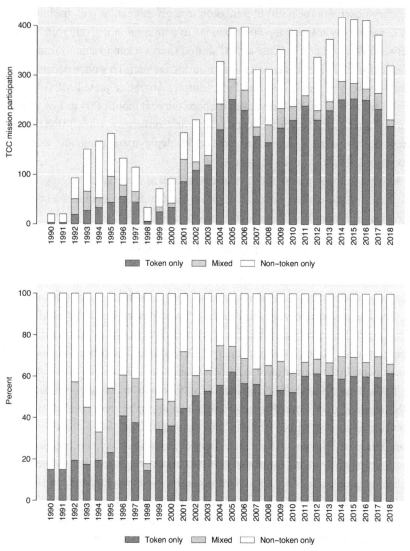

Figure 4 Three modes of mission participation over time
Note: The unit of observation is mission-TCC-year, that is, the mode of troop participation (token only, mixed, and non-token only) of a country for a specific mission in a given year.
Source: UNTFD.

participate in UN peacekeeping (Perry & Smith, 2013). The number of TCCs in major UN operations nearly doubled, from 57 in 1999 to 101 in 2005. The total number of troop contributions reached the previous decade's peak in 2001 and more than doubled by 2005. The share of token contributions also rose sharply, from 35% in 1999 to its highest of 64% in 2005, with a commensurate decline in non-token contributions from 51% to 26%. These figures then stabilized, with slight fluctuations as a result of changes in the active missions. In 2018, the last year for which the IPI data are available,[12] 117 TCCs made 321 contributions to seven active missions; 62% of these were token forces, 34% were non-token deployments, and the remainder were mixed. In short, token forces have become increasingly common over time, emerging as the dominant form of troop contribution in UN peace operations in the early 2000s.

Token Forces by Mission

In addition to increasing in the aggregate, token forces have become ubiquitous across major UN missions. To demonstrate this, we aggregate the country-mission-year data to the mission level by averaging the TCCs' participation modes for a mission in a given year. The resulting measure is a mission's degree of "tokenism" in a particular year, which we can then track over time. Since the tokenism measures at the country-mission-year level range from zero (non-token) to one (token), the measures of mission tokenism are also bound between zero and one. Four missions (MINURCA, UNDOF, UNIFIL, and UNTMIH) have logged a score of zero at some point during their lifespan, with all TCCs making non-token contributions. The maximum value observed is 0.977, which occurred in UNISFA between 2011 and 2018, as Ethiopia was the *only* non-token troop contributor out of about three dozen TCCs. Note that our coding scheme precludes a score of one, in which all TCCs are token troop contributors.

Figure 5 plots the tokenism measures for all 35 missions in the UNTFD over time. Each cell represents a mission's level of tokenism in a given year, from non-token (light gray) to token (black). Neutral colored cells indicate a mission was either inactive or had fallen below the 1,000-troop threshold. The figure highlights several trends. First, consistent with the overall pattern reported earlier, token forces have become more common over time. Most of the light grey cells, representing the years in which the majority of a mission's TCCs made non-token contributions, occur between 1990 and 1999 – the average level of tokenism is 0.29 for this period. From 2000 onward, missions increasingly included token forces, as indicated by the incidence of dark gray cells. The average levels of tokenism are 0.54 and 0.61, respectively, in the second (2000–09) and third (2010–18) decades of the dataset.

---

[12] The UN provides the most up-to-date data on peacekeeping personnel. We use 2018 as the end point of the UNTFD because most other control variables used in the empirical analyses are not available for 2019 onwards.

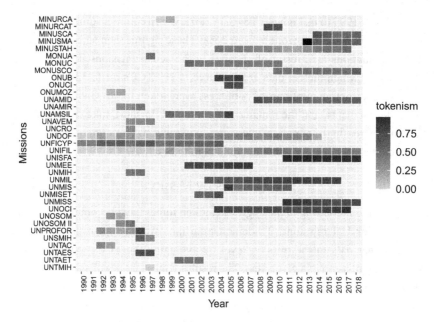

Figure 5 Tokenism in UN peacekeeping missions, 1990–2018
Note: Some active missions (e.g., UNFICYP) are not included for some years because the total number of troops dropped below 1,000.
Source: UNTFD.

Second, token troop contributions remain common across missions' life-spans, despite different operational requirements at mission start-up, full deployment, and draw-down. Comparing the level of tokenism of the first and last year in those missions that continued more than one year and ended before 2018 (i.e., were no longer active) reinforces this point: the average level of tokenism among these 25 missions is 0.5 in the first year and 0.53 in the last year of the mission.

Third, as the phenomenon of token forces has taken hold, missions deployed more recently are more likely to involve a large share of token force contributors at the outset. This becomes more apparent when we examine missions' tokenism levels in the first year they feature in our dataset. Figure 6 presents the resulting scatterplot. All missions that entered the UNTFD in the early 1990s initially had less than half of their TCCs contributing token forces. As time progressed, more missions were initiated with more token than non-token troop contributors. In the last decade, most missions started off with over 60% of TCCs contributing token forces.

Relatedly, some of the older missions started seeing more token forces over time. One exemplary case is UNIFIL. Established in 1978, the mission enters

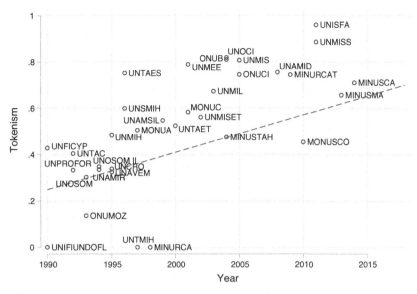

Figure 6 Tokenism of missions in the first year
Note: Each dot represents the level of tokenism for a mission in its first year. The three missions established before 1990 are excluded. The dashed line is the linear fit.
Source: UNTFD.

our dataset in 1990 with nine non-token TCCs (Fiji, Finland, France, Ghana, Ireland, Italy, Nepal, Norway, and Sweden), each contributing an average of 648 troops. The dominance of non-token contributions continued in the next eight years with three additional TCCs that each contributed more than 40 troops (Estonia and Poland) or 10 observers (Zambia), but began to attenuate in 1999 when Denmark, Greece, and Singapore entered the mission with a handful of military observers each.[13] Over the next five years, some of the original participating TCCs (including Fiji, Finland, Ireland, Nepal, and Sweden) decreased their contributions from non-token to token levels, while new non-token contributors such as India and Ukraine emerged. The level of tokenism hovered between 0.08 and 0.25. In 2006, a sea change occurred. The United Nations Interim Force in Lebanon received a much more robust mandate and expanded its total deployment from 2,000 to 6,300 troops. As the number of UNIFIL TCCs quadrupled from 7 to 28, new entrants included both non-token troop contributors (e.g., Bulgaria, China, Denmark, Germany, Indonesia, Malaysia, the Netherlands, Turkey) and token contributors, such as Guatemala (one troop), Hungary (two), Luxemburg (three), Qatar (35), and

---

[13] The United Kingdom joined the mission with 11 military observers, narrowly edging into the non-token category.

Slovenia (11). Three new TCCs (Belgium, Portugal, and Spain) made mixed contributions, all moving from token to non-token, with token contributions occurring in the very first month of their troop deployment. This brought the level of tokenism in UNIFIL to 0.28, and it continued to rise in subsequent years as more token than non-token TCCs joined the mission, including Armenia, Belarus, Brazil, Brunei, Colombia, Croatia, Cyprus, East Timor, Kenya, Macedonia, Mexico, the Netherlands, Niger, Nigeria, Serbia, Sierra Leone, Slovakia, Slovenia, South Korea, and Uruguay. Between 2008 and 2018, the average level of tokenism in UNIFIL reached 0.4, as represented by the dark gray cells in Figure 5.

In short, Figure 5 illustrates that tokenism has become common across all major UN peace operations. Remarkably, this ubiquity appears to extend across the full range of conflict environments. It would be plausible to expect the contrary. On the one hand, the UN might only accept token forces in low-risk missions, and/or states may prefer to send substantial units capable of self-defense to riskier operations. On the other hand, countries might be more willing to send large contingents to relatively safe missions and reserve token forces for deadlier ones. Taking a first stab at investigating these possible correlations further, we use the UN peacekeeping fatalities dataset (Henke, 2019) as a proxy for the degree of danger in the missions. Specifically, we gather the number of total fatalities caused by accidents, illness, malicious acts (i.e., hostilities), and other incident types for each mission in the dataset.

In total, the 35 missions in the UNTFD have suffered 2,763 fatalities, with an average of 86 and a standard deviation of 82, indicating huge variation across the missions. The most dangerous missions for peacekeepers as measured by fatalities are UNAMID (278), UNPROFOR (213), MINUSMA (209), UNMIL (204), UNAMSIL (192), MINUSTAH (187), MONUSCO (186), MONUC (161), UNOSOM (160), and UNOCI (151).[14] The average level of tokenism of these 10 missions is 0.49, compared to 0.48 for the 10 safest missions. Further illustrating the lack of distinction, the missions in Cyprus and in the Golan Heights are both relatively safe, with 30 fatalities each, but tokenism in UNDOF (0.26) is less than half of tokenism in UNFICYP (0.54). Overall, token troop contributions appear to be similarly common across more and less dangerous missions. Figure 7 plots the relationship between mission fatalities and tokenism rates. The coefficient of correlation is −0.05, and the linear fit is practically a straight line, suggesting that the incidence of token forces is not correlated with a mission's conflict environment.

---

[14] MINUSMA is currently said to be the most dangerous UN mission. The large number of fatalities in MINUSTAH is primarily driven by the 2010 Haiti earthquake, which caused 100 UN fatalities.

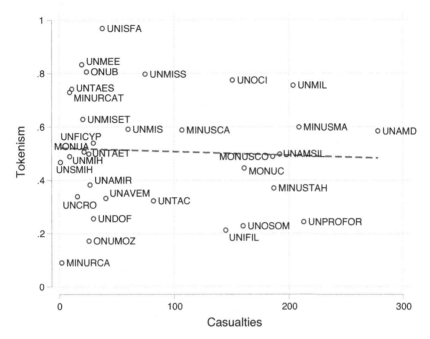

Figure 7 Mission tokenism and casualties
Note: Each dot represents the average level of tokenism (*y*-axis) and the cumulative number of fatalities (*x*-axis) for each mission covered in the time span of the dataset. The dashed line is the linear fit.
Source: UNTFD.

Token Forces by Troop-Contributing Country

To complete our investigation of the ubiquity of token forces in UN peacekeeping, we now turn to the TCC level and demonstrate that tokenism has become widespread across UN troop contributors. Similar to the construction of our mission-level tokenism measure, we aggregate the country-mission-year observations for all the missions in which a TCC participated in a given year. This aggregation results in 2,570 country-year observations, each of which can be understood as one TCC's portfolio of troop contributions in a given year. The value of this measure ranges from zero (non-token troop contributions only) to one (token troop contributions only). Any value between zero and one indicates mixed contributions, where a TCC made token troop contributions to some missions and non-token ones to others; the more token contributions relative to non-token ones, the closer the measure is to one.

Figure 8 plots the tokenism measure for each TCC, averaged across the 29-year period. The average level of tokenism is 0.59, with a standard deviation of

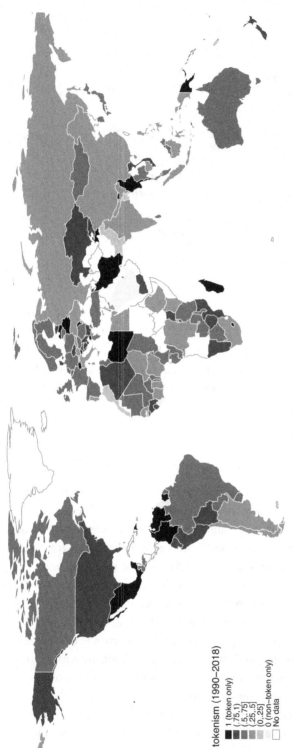

Figure 8 TCC tokenism, 1990–2018

tokenism (1990–2018)
- 1 (token only)
- (.75,1)
- (.5,.75]
- (.25,.5]
- (0,.25]
- 0 (non–token only)
- No data

Source: UNTFD.

0.36, suggesting wide variation across the countries. However, only four TCCs (Kuwait, Liberia, Saudi Arabia, and United Arab Emirates) belong to the "non-token-only" category for all the years they contributed troops, and of these states, only Liberia participated in UN peacekeeping after 2000. Thus, virtually all UN TCCs over the past two decades have made at least one token troop contribution to a major UN mission. Thirty TCCs belong to the "token-only" category for all the years they contributed troops, led by Switzerland (19 missions), Bhutan (8), Moldova (7), Slovenia (4), and Iran (3). The vast majority of TCCs thus have mixed portfolios of token and non-token troop contributions in any given year; 71% of these TCCs made more token than non-token troop contributions over our period of observation (tokenism >0.5), represented by darker shades of gray in the map.

To explore how countries' contribution portfolios evolved over time, Figure 9 plots the incidence of TCCs making token-only, mixed, and non-token-only contributions by year, in aggregate numbers and as a share of the total number of TCCs. Similar to the patterns in Figure 4, the incidence of countries making only token troop contributions increases over time, in both absolute and relative terms, while the incidence of TCCs only contributing non-token forces declines. Unlike in Figure 4, the mixed deployment portfolio is the dominant category in 24 out of 29 years. In other words, the majority of TCCs make token troop contributions to some missions and non-token contributions to others in any given year, confirming that token participation is typically a deliberate policy decision with respect to a particular mission rather than a result of absolute resource constraints (Coleman, 2013).

To verify how widespread tokenism has become among UN TCCs – beyond the geographical diversity illustrated in Figure 8 – we examine the relationship between token troop contributions and four key country-specific characteristics averaged across the 29-year period. The first one is the level of economic development measured by GDP per capita. Second, we consider average financial contributions to UN peacekeeping as a measure of UN influence.[15] Our third measure is Polity IV regime type, ranging from −10 for highly autocratic states to +10 for highly democratic ones (Marshall & Gurr, 2014). Finally, we use the size of national armed forces as a proxy for troop availability.

Figure 10 presents the scatterplots of TCC tokenism in relation to the four measures. Also plotted are the lines of linear fit, with slopes all close to zero. The coefficients of correlation range from −0.02 to 0.08.[16] Overall, these results

---

[15] The financial contribution database was last updated in March 2016.

[16] The USA is a potential outlier, given its massive GDP and financial contribution to UN peacekeeping. Removing it pulls the line of linear fit downward, though the slopes remain statistically insignificant in simple bivariate regressions.

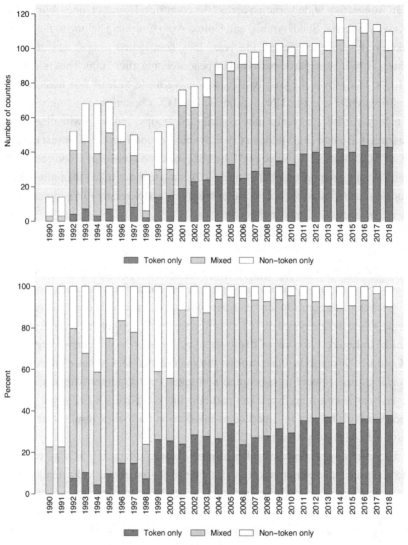

Figure 9 TCC deployment portfolios, 1990–2018
Note: The unit of observation is TCC-year, that is, portfolio of troop participation
(token only, mixed, and non-token only) of a country for all the missions in which
it participated in a given year.
Source: UNTFD.

suggest that a wide range of TCCs make token troop contributions, and their
deployment portfolios are not driven by ostensible differences in economic
development, financial resources, domestic institutions, or armed forces size.
Both large and small countries make token troop contributions, as do both

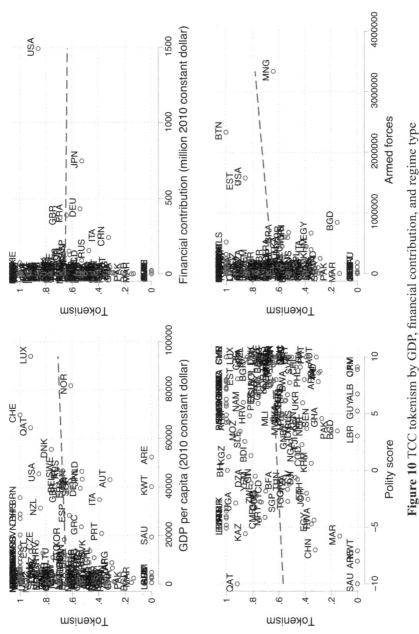

Figure 10 TCC tokenism by GDP, financial contribution, and regime type

Source: World Development Indicators (WDI), Polity IV Project, IPI Peacekeeping Database, and UNTFD.

democracies and autocracies. Neither a state's financial contribution to UN peacekeeping nor the size of its armed forces affect its likelihood of sending token forces.[17]

Conclusion

This section has provided the first systematic overview of the emergence and evolution of token forces in UN peace operations. The empirical data over the past three decades bear out the claim that token troop contributions are a significant, distinctive, and increasingly common form of participation in UN peace operations. Using data covering the universe of TCCs from 1990 to 2018, we document that token forces are common in UN peacekeeping overall, widespread among troop contributors, ubiquitous across missions, persistent over mission life spans, and increasingly common over time. These overall patterns provide more context for Sections 3 and 4, which investigate the phenomenon of token forces from the perspectives of TCCs and the UN, respectively.

3 The Diffusion of Token Participation among UN Troop Contributors

In this section, we examine token forces from the point of view of TCCs. We begin by exploring why states may consider token forces a more attractive option for participating in a particular UN mission than either a substantial troop deployment or nonparticipation. We then conceptualize diffusion through learning as a key mechanism through which states gradually recognized that token participation in UN peace operations is a viable policy option for them: countries learn from other states' troop deployments as well as their own experience what types of contributions they can make to UN peacekeeping. Finally, we present our research design, the construction of our diffusion measures, and our empirical evidence of diffusion.

State Motivations for Contributing Token Forces

Compared to more substantial troop deployments, token forces have four potential disadvantages for the contributing state. They do not establish the state as a major troop contributor able to claim prestige and a share of the mission's senior staff officer positions.[18] They do not permit the TCC to

---

[17] We argue in Section 4, however, that states making large financial contributions to UN peacekeeping typically make a different type of token contribution (senior staff officers) than less influential TCCs.

[18] See Section 4 for further discussion.

autonomously contribute to the mission's military operations. They limit the number of personnel gaining operational experience from the deployment. They also generate limited income for states whose deployment costs are below UN reimbursement rates: "if [states] are financially driven then they want either a unit that has lots of people – because people pays – or lots of equipment, because equipment pays" (UN_HQ12).

However, token forces also present significant advantages relative to larger deployments. First, they limit the TCC's military and political risk, both because it has fewer troops deployed and because staff officers, military observers, and most co-deployed troops[19] serve in nonkinetic roles. Second, token forces are less resource intensive to deploy than substantial military units. Some TCCs report having insufficient personnel to deploy substantial contingents, often due to competing domestic needs (e.g., "We need every single soldier to protect our borders," UN_PK9) or other international deployments (UN_PK19, UN_PK7, UN_PK42, UN_PK11). For others, meeting UN equipment and self-sustainment requirements is a major constraint (UN_HQ17) and these do not apply to individually deployed staff officers and military observers (Coleman, 2013) and are typically assumed by the larger TCC in the case of co-deployed contingent troops (UN_PK6; also Daniel et al., 2015). Finally, for the growing number of states whose deployment costs exceed UN reimbursement rates (Coleman & Nyblade, 2018), token forces minimize the financial cost of participating in UN peacekeeping.

Compared to nonparticipation in a mission, token forces present an array of benefits. They provide the TCC with inside information about the operation, particularly if the contribution includes military observers (who monitor mission progress in their area of deployment) or staff officers, who, depending on their seniority, have higher-level operational information. One MONUSCO military observer noted, "Of course, I inform my government of what is going on in this mission and I hope this information will come to our permanent representors in New York" (UN_PK27). Another concurred, "I'm also ... something like a source of information for my country ... from the exact theater" (UN_PK45). Similarly, for an UNFICYP peacekeeper, "having me here providing insight into what UNFICYP is doing allows our ambassador in Greece to be made aware of the situation, instead of just getting it third and fourth hand."[20] Token contributions of senior staff officers allow states to wield considerable operational influence: "You don't need a large number of people to have influence in a mission. . . . You can have a disproportionate effect with one

---

[19] We return to this point in Section 4.
[20] Remark not for further attribution, even in anonymized form.

or two people. You can have influence in terms of steering the mission in a particular direction" (UN_PK12). Co-deployed token contingent troops, meanwhile, present opportunities to strengthen political ties and improve military interoperability among the partnering TCCs:

> It is not [primarily] a military reason, but relations between countries. Just to ensure that there is mutual trust between the countries ... we also achieve the trust between militaries. But ... [t]he main issue is ... to improve the relationship, the mutual trust and confidence between countries. (UN_PK34)

In addition, all token forces – regardless of type – allow the contributing state to claim the political benefits of participation in UN peacekeeping. One benefit is having a voice in UN discussions related to the mission:

> As long as there is a [national] contribution, [our] ambassador to the UN goes to all the meetings, is privy to all the information, and has a say in what happens with the mission. Whether your contingent is a thousand or it's one, you still have a voice. (UN_PK32)

A second benefit is the ability to demonstrate UN engagement to domestic publics that may favor UN peacekeeping but not necessarily support costly deployments or be overly aware of contribution size (UN_PK15). Finally, even token participation in a UN peace operation signals good global citizenship. As a UNFICYP peacekeeper put it,

> nations want to participate in international peace operations for political reasons ... to show good will to the host state and of course to demonstrate to the UN [our] readiness to send soldiers to different international missions, even if it is only a small contribution. (UN_PK33)

Members of MONUSCO's token forces agreed. For one, "We are showing [our] flag. We have [our nationals] in Africa. Maybe just a few, but we are making a contribution" (UN_PK55). For another, "I think the intention is to show ourselves and show that we are also contributing – but of course, only with individual specialists, right, because [we] can't send a thousand or two thousand soldiers" (UN_PK64). A third concurred that their deployment served "at least at the minimum level to show our participation in MONUSCO" (UN_PK45). In short, "it's in the interest of the nation to be able to fly their flag and say, hey, we are here, too. Of course that's an important point, every state has an interest in that" (UN_PK43).

Thus, while nonparticipation remains a frequent choice, multiple factors make token forces a potentially attractive alternative for states that are unwilling or unable to make a substantial troop contribution to a particular UN mission. To act on such preferences for token over nonparticipation, however, states had to recognize – or learn – that token troop contributions were a politically viable policy option.

Diffusion: Learning about Token Participation

International diffusion occurs when government policy decisions in one country are systematically shaped by policy choices made in other states (Simmons et al., 2006). In general, diffusion can take place within and across countries, among both public and private actors, and can lead to the spread of a wide range of entities, such as instruments, standards, and institutions (Gilardi, 2012). In the context of International Relations, diffusion often occurs at the country level, pertaining to broad policy models (e.g., market reforms), ideational frameworks (e.g., the nuclear taboo), and institutional settings (e.g., democratic institutions). For our purposes, we are interested in the diffusion of the practice of token troop contributions across time and space, leading to the increased deployment of such forces among TCCs documented in Section 2.

How does diffusion occur? International Relations scholars have identified four main mechanisms: coercion, the "imposition of a policy by powerful international organizations or countries"; competition, where "countries influenc[e] one another to try to attract economic resources"; learning, whereby "the experience of other countries can supply useful information on the likely consequences of a policy"; and emulation, when "the normative and socially constructed characteristics of policies matter more than their objective consequences" (Gilardi, 2012, p. 461). In the case of UN token forces, learning is the most plausible diffusion mechanism, since TCCs are not forced to deploy token forces, and states competing to secure economic resources would primarily aim to deploy non-token contributions. Emulation is possible, but since (as noted in Section 1) there is no general international norm enjoining token over substantial contributions, this requires learning that tokenism – or a particular form of tokenism – is associated with a set of states the potential TCC recognizes as having high status.

Central to the learning mechanism is the notion that when a new policy option emerges, there is generally limited information about its feasibility and likely consequences. Thus, policy makers observe other countries' experiences as well as monitoring the results of any initial policy trials by their own country, to evaluate the viability and likely effects of adoption. This process may involve fully rational Bayesian updating (Gilardi, 2012), where policy makers revise their prior beliefs about the consequences and/or feasibility of a policy or practice based on information coming from all other countries as well as any direct national experience, though the extent of adaptation depends on the consistency of the information and the strength of policy makers' prior beliefs. Learning can also be bounded, in the sense that not all information will be considered equally, as policy makers may use cognitive shortcuts such as "availability" and "representativeness" when trying to make sense of information in uncertain circumstances (McDermott, 2001). Thus, experiences of some countries (e.g., neighboring countries, more powerful states) may have a disproportionately large influence on learning.

Multiple early studies of diffusion by learning demonstrate that countries do use the experiences of others to inform their own decisions on policy adoption. Elkins et al. (2006) show that countries are more likely to sign bilateral investment treaties if the experience of others in the region and the world indicates this policy leads to the desired outcome. Meseguer (2009) finds that the adoption of market reforms is significantly influenced by how policy makers perceive their expected consequences for economic growth, based on other countries' experiences. Gilardi et al. (2009) show that health care reforms are more likely to be adopted by OECD countries if the experience of others suggests they are correlated with decreased expenditures.

Building on these works, more recent studies have used spatial dependence and geographical proximity to study diffusions of human rights practices (Greenhill, 2010), democratic regimes (Zhukov & Stewart, 2013), the responsibility to protect norm (Acharya, 2013), same-sex marriage recognition (Mitchell & Petray, 2016), Arab Spring protests (Weyland, 2012), and NGO restriction (Glasius et al., 2020). Drawing on insights from these studies, we hypothesize that TCCs learn from other countries as well as their own experiences and direct communication with UN officials which types of forces they can contribute to UN peace operations. This learning can take two broad forms, which are not mutually exclusive. First, states can observe other states' troop contributions, not least through the detailed monthly data the UN releases, which states pay close attention to: "if you forget one individual, the member state immediately calls!" (UN_HQ5). Second, diplomats from states' permanent missions to the UN routinely interact with each other (Pouliot, 2016, Chapter 5) and can exchange information about their intended contributions (or negotiate a joint contribution) during the force-generation process for a mission and at subsequent meetings for mission TCCs if the force structure is being adjusted. Such exchanges often occur on a regional basis, as suggested by one UN Headquarters official:

> [T]he community of the [states'] military advisors always have their own agenda, their own meetings, by missions, social events ... [and] region. I know that there are some groups, for instance the group of South America, the group of Asia, the group of non-Aligned, the group of – they have different groups. They are working all together, but there are different groups, just to share in common (UN_HQ4).

Thus, states have ample opportunity to learn from each other both during the force-generation process and by observing its outcomes. As more countries – and perhaps especially similar countries – deploy token forces, state decision makers learn about the feasibility of token participation in UN operations, increasing the likelihood that they too will seek to deploy token forces.

Research Design

Our sample consists of 151 countries that have contributed to UN peacekeeping at least once from 1990 to 2018. The dependent variable is a country's mode of participation in a given year. There are four possible outcomes: (1) no participation in any UN operations; (2) token participation only; (3) mixed participation (token in some missions and non-token in others); (4) non-token participation only. Of the 4,379 (151×29) country-year observations, nearly half (46.7%) are no participation. Where states do participate in UN peacekeeping, mixed participation is most common (30% of total observations, see also Figure 9), followed by token-only participation (15.5%) and non-token-only participation (7.8%).

Measuring Diffusion

For both qualitative and quantitative researchers, the starting point for measuring diffusion is to identify the spatial and/or temporal clustering, such as neighboring countries adopting similar policies, or an adoption pattern characterized by waves. In operationalization, scholars have used a broad range of criteria to determine how distance is expected to affect influence, reflecting the diversity of phenomena being measured. Since we are interested in the diffusion of token troop contributions, which occur in two of the four possible outcomes of our dependent variable, we employ two distance-based measures that are weighted sums of token-only and mixed participation observed in neighboring countries.

To do so, we first create a row-standardized connectivity matrix **W**. Each element of the matrix is $w_{ij} = \frac{c_{ij}}{\sum_{j=1}^{n} c_{ij}}$, where c_{ij} equals 1 if countries i and j are connected. For our purposes, we define a country's neighborhood through land and water contiguity (Stinnett et al., 2002), where the connectivity condition is satisfied if the borders of two countries intersect through either a land boundary or a river, or when a straight line of no more than 400 miles can be drawn between a point on the border of one state, across open water (uninterrupted by the territory of a third state), to the closest point on the homeland territory of another state.

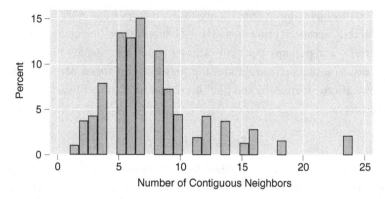

Figure 11 Number of neighboring countries
Source: UNTFD.

Figure 11 displays the distribution of contiguous neighbors for all countries in the sample. The mode is 7 and the mean is 7.8. Twelve countries are contiguous to only one neighbor (in parentheses): Canada (USA), Cape Verde (Senegal), Gambia (Senegal), Lesotho (South Africa), Madagascar (India), Marshall Islands (Kiribati), Mauritius (Seychelles), Nauru (Kiribati), Samoa (Tonga), San Marino (Italy), Sri Lanka (India), and Vanuatu (Solomon Islands). Russia has the largest number of contiguous neighbors (24): Azerbaijan, Belarus, Bulgaria, China, Denmark, Estonia, Finland, Germany, Greece, Japan, Kazakhstan, Latvia, Lithuania, Mongolia, North Korea, Norway, Poland, Romania, South Korea, Sweden, Turkey, Turkmenistan, Ukraine, and the USA.

Next, we use the spatial weighting matrix to construct the ratio of a country's neighbors deploying either token forces only or a mix of contributions (e.g., token in some missions and non-token in others) in a given year. These values are calculated as $\sum_{j=1}^{n} w_{ij} t_{j}$, where w_{ij} is an element of the row-standardized spatial weights matrix $\mathbf{W}$ defined earlier and t_j is a binary indicator that takes the value of 1 if country j sent only token forces or a mix of token and non-token forces to the peacekeeping operations it participated in that year, and zero otherwise.

Model Specification

Since the dependent variable contains four distinct outcomes, we use multinomial logistic regression, which is akin to running three independent binary logistic regression models with "no participation" as the baseline and the other three outcomes separately regressed against the baseline outcome. The key independent variables are the two spatially weighted measures of tokenism as well as the global trend of tokenism.[21] In addition, we include a battery of country-, mission-, and host-specific control variables to account for other potential explanations for the different modes of participation.

First, we include several measures to account for domestic resources for troop deployment, including total armed forces personnel, GDP per capita, and population. States with more military personnel are known to be more likely to intervene in civil violence, provide peacekeeping, and protect civilians (Mueller, 2004) and may be more likely to send substantial troop contributions simply because they can better afford them. Similarly, more populous states have more people to potentially contribute non-token forces to peacekeeping missions. Poorer states are more likely to participate in UN peacekeeping to help fund their militaries (e.g., Victor, 2010; Bove & Elia, 2011; but see Coleman & Nyblade, 2018), and (as noted earlier) may therefore prefer substantial to token deployments. All three measures are drawn from the WDI (World Bank, 2021), with GDP and population data supplemented by the Penn World Tables (Feenstra et al., 2015). We use log transformation to smooth the highly skewed distribution of these measures.

Second, extant scholarship on peacekeeping contributions often suggests that regime type shapes a state's UN troop deployment decisions. Some scholars argue democratic governments are more likely than nondemocratic leaders to support peacekeeping because they have an ideational commitment to diffusing liberal institutions (Andersson, 2000; Lebovic, 2004; Perkins & Neumayer, 2008; Raes et al., 2019), while others find democracies are less likely to deploy substantial contingents because of popular risk aversion (Duursma & Gledhill, 2019). To account for either mechanism, we include each TCC's regime type using its Polity score as described in Section 2.

Third, multiple studies suggest that military deployments will be more acceptable to domestic publics if the risk of casualties is low (Cook, 2000; Gartner, 2008; Gelpi et al., 2009). Thus, we include a measure of mission death, drawing on the same source as in Section 2 (Henke, 2019) but focusing on the 530 fatalities due to malicious acts only. The measure is highly skewed; 74 countries in the dataset never experienced any fatalities and another 24 only one fatality. Chad (41), Pakistan (32), and the USA (30) suffered the highest number of fatalities. Notably, nearly all of Pakistan's fatalities occurred in UNOSOM between June and September 1993.

Fourth, it may be the case that a state currently hosting a peace operation is unlikely or unable to contribute troops to ongoing missions elsewhere.

---

[21] In the Appendix Table A2, we report findings using measures constructed with spatial weighting matrices based on regions.

We therefore include a dichotomous indicator of whether a state is currently hosting a mission included in the UNTFD (Kathman, 2013).

Fifth, we include the total number of ongoing missions in the world in a given year to control for there being more missions available for countries to join in some years than others, though this could also make countries more selective. We also control for the number of ongoing missions in the TCC's own region, since regional solidarity norms and/or conflict spillover effects may provide additional motivations for states to participate in an operation and perhaps to offer substantial rather than token contributions (Bove & Elia, 2011; Kathman, 2013). Since all the missions in our data occur in Africa, Asia, Europe, or South America, this measure is zero for countries in North America and Oceania.

Sixth, characteristics of the host countries may also matter when a TCC decides what types of force to deploy. Thus, we include the regime type, population, and GDP per capita of the host countries of all active missions in a given year. As before, the population and GDP per capita measures are taken from the WDI and log transformed.

Finally, we account for potential path dependency by including the participation mode of the country in the previous year, measured as three dummy variables corresponding to token troop participation, mixed participation, and non-token troop participation. Including these lags helps alleviate potential problems of autocorrelation in the data and controls for the fact that most missions last multiple years, so states may continue to participate, possibly deploying the same types of forces, in missions where they have already invested resources and labor. These measures also capture the possibility that states are learning from their own experiences and from other states over time.[22]

Findings

Table 1 presents the results from the full model that includes neighbor token and mixed participations as well as the control variables. There are three columns labeled with the three outcomes (token, mixed, and non-token troop participations) with nonparticipation as the reference category. For each outcome, a positive coefficient indicates that a unit increase in the independent variable increases the likelihood that a country will contribute in that way relative to not contributing any troops in a given year.

Focusing on neighboring countries' token troop contributions first, we see that the coefficients are statistically significant across all three equations. Token

---

[22] In the Appendix Table A3, we present findings from a model without the lagged participation variables and with the diffusion measures lagged one year. The results are similar to those reported in Table 1.

Table 1 Determinants of mode of participation in UN peacekeeping operations

Variable	Token force	Mixed	Non-token force
Neighbor token force participation	4.822**	2.276*	−2.270**
	(0.885)	(0.902)	(0.666)
Neighbor mixed participation	1.261	5.085**	−1.510**
	(0.845)	(0.776)	(0.388)
Armed forces personnel (logged)	−0.119	-0.148	−0.0398
	(0.123)	(0.137)	(0.125)
Population (logged)	0.324*	0.561**	0.501**
	(0.140)	(0.169)	(0.143)
GDP per capita (logged)	0.247*	0.0572	0.136
	(0.0985)	(0.0847)	(0.0775)
Polity score	0.0407*	0.0626**	0.0679**
	(0.0182)	(0.0214)	(0.0180)
Host	−1.687**	−2.363**	−0.701
	(0.551)	(0.574)	(0.605)
Casualty	−0.144	0.785	0.752
	(0.519)	(0.470)	(0.474)
Ongoing mission, global	−0.228*	−0.317**	−0.220**
	(0.0915)	(0.0711)	(0.0785)
Ongoing mission, regional	0.113*	0.0773	0.165**
	(0.0549)	(0.0558)	(0.0628)
Mission hosts polity scores	−0.268*	−0.458**	−0.524**
	(0.122)	(0.117)	(0.118)
Mission hosts population (logged)	0.193	−0.375**	−0.198
	(0.192)	(0.139)	(0.194)
Mission hosts GDP per capita (logged)	−1.547**	−1.761**	−1.866**
	(0.387)	(0.382)	(0.357)
Token force participation $(t-1)$	4.668**	3.979**	0.655
	(0.253)	(0.302)	(0.650)
Mixed participation $(t-1)$	3.282**	6.608**	3.896**
	(0.274)	(0.332)	(0.324)
Non-token participation $(t-1)$	1.206*	4.408**	4.611**
	(0.491)	(0.323)	(0.278)
Constant	−0.696	6.812	7.722
	(5.368)	(4.644)	(4.516)

Table 1 (cont.)

Variable	Token force	Mixed	Non-token force
Observations	3,621	3,621	3,621
Pseudo R-squared	0.618	0.618	0.618
Chi squared	2907	2907	2907
Log likelihood	−1719	−1719	−1719

Note: Robust standard errors clustered by country in parentheses. ** p <0.01, * p <0.05

forces from neighboring countries increase the likelihood that the state will send token forces or a mix of token and non-token contributions relative to not sending any troops. In contrast, token troop contributions by neighboring countries decrease the state's inclination to send non-token forces.

Figure 12 plots the predicted probabilities as a function of token forces from neighboring countries for the four outcomes. The predicted probabilities are calculated using estimates from Table 1, with the other variables held at their mean, and they add up to one at any given ratio of neighboring countries sending token forces. The probability that a country participates in UN peacekeeping missions with only token forces is practically zero when none of its neighbors are doing that. Instead, there is a 50% chance that the country is not participating in any missions, followed by mixed participation (30%) and non-token-only participation (18%).

As the ratio of neighboring countries deploying token forces only increases, the probability that the country will follow suit increases in tandem, while the likelihood of nonparticipation and non-token contributions decreases. The probability of mixed participation, however, initially increases slightly, and then starts to drop after the ratio of neighborhood tokenism reaches 0.5. At the other end of the continuum, where all the neighboring countries contribute token forces only, the likelihood of a state making a token force contribution is over 70%, followed by mixed participation at about 20%, while the probabilities of the other two outcomes approach zero.

The effects of mixed participation from neighboring countries are similar – the coefficient estimates in Table 1 have the same sign, though with different magnitudes, and two of them are statistically significant. Mixed participation by neighbors increases the likelihood of mixed participation as well but decreases the likelihood of non-token participation. Figure 13 similarly plots the predicted probabilities as a function of neighbor mixed participation. Moving from no mixed participation to mixed participation by every neighbor increases the

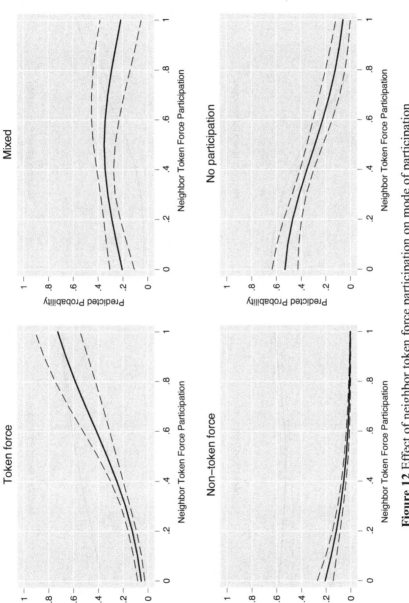

Figure 12 Effect of neighbor token force participation on mode of participation

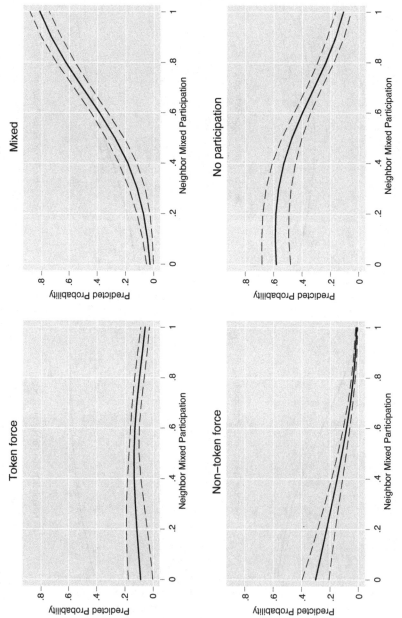

Figure 13 Effect of neighbor mixed participation on mode of participation

likelihood of mixed participation from nearly zero to over 80%. Taken together, these results point to a diffusion mechanism whereby TCCs learn from geographically proximate countries about the token force option and adopt the same practice over time.

We now turn to the control variables in the model. Of the three measures of capacity, the number of armed forces personnel does not have any significant effects on the mode of participation. More populous countries are more likely than ones with smaller populations to engage in each of the three modes of participation, but unsurprisingly, the effect is smallest for token force contributions. Richer countries prefer to deploy token forces rather than no troops but are no more inclined to send more than that. This finding is consistent with existing research (e.g., Duursma & Gledhill, 2019) and may have several causes. First, rich countries may see their larger UN financial contributions as a substitute for large deployments (UN_PK8) and/or may opt to channel their peacekeeping contributions through non-UN operations (Bellamy & Williams, 2009; Gaibulloev et al., 2009). Furthermore, their governments have a financial disincentive to contribute large peacekeeping contingents, since their deployment costs typically exceed UN reimbursement rates (Gaibulloev et al., 2015, p. 730).

In terms of domestic politics, fatalities in peacekeeping missions do not significantly affect states' choice of participation mode in UN missions, but being a PKO host country reduces the likelihood of both token and mixed participations, a finding consistent with prior studies. Conversely, more-democratic countries prefer all three modes to not contributing any troops. This supports the general consensus in the literature (e.g., Victor, 2010; Gaibulloev et al., 2015; Ward & Dorussen, 2016; Duursma & Gledhill, 2019) that leaders of democratic regimes are particularly willing to contribute troops to peacekeeping operations to externalize their domestic norms of peace (Lebovic, 2004) or to please humanitarian factions within their state (Jakobsen, 1996; Western, 2002).

The two measures of existing PKO missions in the world and the same region as the TCC have opposite effects. More concurrent missions globally decrease all three modes of troop contribution, exerting the largest effect on mixed participation. This lends support to the idea that countries face a "troops constraint" (Bove & Elia, 2011): when the number of operations being sustained at any one time increases, it becomes harder for countries to join additional operations. In contrast, the number of missions in the same region has a significant and positive effect on token and non-token contributions, indicating that geographic proximity to the conflict region bolsters the chances of peacekeeping contributions to that region.

All three measures of a host state's characteristics matter – countries are less likely to deploy troops in any mode to more-democratic and richer hosts, and to send a mix of token and non-token forces to more populous countries.[23]

Finally, all the lagged modes of contribution are positively correlated with increased likelihood of troop contributions, with the notable exception – which we turn to in Section 4 – that token force contribution in the previous year is not associated with increased likelihood of non-token contributions. Furthermore, the substantive effects of the lagged contribution modes are the largest for the same mode of contribution, suggesting that while countries do shift among different modes of deployment, there is strong path dependency and/or self-learning for continued contributions in the same manner over time.

Conclusion

This section set out to understand in more detail the motivations behind countries choosing to deploy token forces as a distinct alternative to either substantial deployment or nonparticipation. Token forces can be an attractive option, requiring fewer resources and imposing less risk than larger deployments, and generating more prestige, operational influence and knowledge, and deployment experiences than nonparticipation. To reap these benefits, however, states must be aware that the opportunity for token participation in UN peace operations exists, both in general and for them in particular. We hypothesize that a process of diffusion by learning helped drive the increased incidence of token forces over time, as countries learned about the opportunity for token participation in part by observing other states deploy token forces.

Using proximity-based measures of diffusion, our empirical analyses lent strong support to this hypothesis. In particular, we found that countries learn from those in close geographical proximity. When more countries in the neighborhood deploy token forces, whether in all missions in which they participate or in conjunction with larger deployments, the likelihood of a state contributing token forces increases. These results are robust to the inclusion of other country-, mission-, and host-specific factors, many of which are consistent with findings from existing studies.

4 Token Forces from the UN's Perspective

Having examined the rise of token forces from the point of view of contributing countries, we now turn to the UN's perspective. States can only deploy to a UN operation if the UN accepts their troop contribution. Why do UN coalition

---

[23] These effects should not be extrapolated beyond the limited range of the values in these measures from 22 host countries in the dataset.

builders welcome token forces, and how have they accommodated – and shaped – the rise in tokenism over time observed in Sections 2 and 3?

As we suggested in Section 1, in isolation neither legitimacy nor capability-aggregation considerations can fully explain the UN's position. Legitimation does play an important role in explaining UN officials' welcoming of token forces: "Having more and different flags that you would not otherwise have adds to the mission's legitimacy and to the sense that the UN really represents all its member states" (UN_HQ3). In UNFICYP, "We can say that we have troops from 20 member states . . . so it adds to the international character of the operation, rather than if we had only three contributing countries" (UN_PK6*). A MONUSCO official concurred: "the more countries participate, the higher the legitimacy" (UN_PK60*). Overall, as Figure 14 shows, between 1998 and 2018 a 16-fold expansion of the average number of token contributors in a UN operation (from 2.3 to 36) drove a 5-fold increase in the average coalition size, from 9.5 to 52 TCCs. In this sense, token forces contributed significantly to long-standing UN efforts to "expand the base" of UN troop contributors (UNDPKO & UNDFS, 2009, p. vi).

Yet UN officials are typically sanguine about their operations' international legitimacy: a mission

> is legitimate by virtue of being authorized by the Council. But [if] we could give it a greater degree of plurality . . . it would be seen as being more representative of the member states and not just a part of the member states. (UN_PK66*)

Non-UN coalition builders often see a greater need to recruit even token contributors in order to legitimate their intervention through a broad coalition. For the controversial 2003 US-led Multinational Force in Iraq (MNF-I), coalition builders clearly prioritized legitimacy over capability aggregation: "the inclusion of odds and ends [was] not necessarily conducive to military efficiency, but it [was] a price worth paying for the advantage of the political mandate that it gives" (Iraq_2). As a coalition builder, "they might put you on a plane and you might only get six solders without boots on, but what mattered was getting the flag on the front page."[24] One UN official explicitly contrasted MNF-I with UN practice: "That was definitely tokenism . . . [S]ome countries . . . were there for political reasons, to fly the political flag for the Americans. That's not really the way it is in UN peacekeeping" (UN_HQ11). Unlike MNF-I, ISAF benefited from the legitimacy of a UN mandate, but it also faced accusations of US-dominated aggression that NATO officials sought to address with a broad coalition: "NATO really needs partners, additional partners, to give it legitimacy. Because in the eyes of

---

[24] Professional communication, 2016.

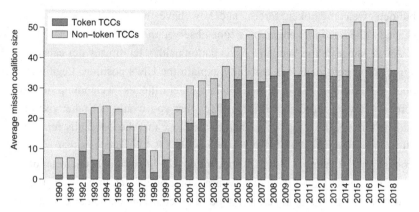

Figure 14 Coalition size by token and non-token TCCs over time
Note: The small number of mixed contributors in a mission (see Figure 4) are reclassified as token or non-token based on their contribution type for the majority of the year.
Source: UNTFD.

the Arab [*sic*] world, NATO ... is Western, American dominated" (ISAF_16). Consequently, ISAF coalition builders would "deliberately keep [contribution size] flexible, because, sometimes, there will be political benefit in actually having a particular country inside the club ... I mean, for example, getting Islamic nations into ISAF was pretty important" (ISAF_6). Nevertheless, at its 2010–12 peak, ISAF had a tokenism rate of 18–24% among its 48–50 coalition members, less than half the contemporaneous UN rate.[25] If UN coalition builders are typically less concerned about their operations' legitimacy than their non-UN counterparts, why would they welcome higher rates of tokenism?

Capability-aggregation considerations cannot answer this question. Token forces furnish only a tiny percentage of total troops deployed in UN missions, as the examples of MONUSCO and MINUSCA in Section 1 suggested and Figure 15 confirms. On average, token forces accounted for 1.16% of deployed UN peace-keepers from 1990 to 2018.[26] At best, token forces pale in comparison to the 17% average monthly troop shortfall (16.7% for military observers) UN missions experienced in 1990–2010 (Passmore et al., 2018, p. 367). At worst, they contributed to this shortfall as states capable of deploying large contingents instead chose token participation (Coleman, 2013). United Nations officials recognized that the apparently "expanding base" of TCCs remained too shallow: "nearly 60% of contributions come from the top 10 countries ... this approach is clearly not

---

[25] Data from NATO placemats, www.nato.int/cps/en/natolive/107995.htm.
[26] See Appendix Figure A1 for variations over time and within each year.

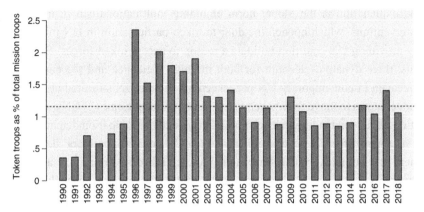

Figure 15 Token troops as percentage of total mission troops by year
Note: The bars represent the percentages of token troops in a mission averaged across all missions each year. The dashed line is the average of this measure across all years.
Source: UNTFD.

sustainable, and the UN must expand both the current pool of contributors *and the scale and range of contributions*" (Ziai, 2009, p. 31 emphasis added). Nevertheless, tokenism plateaued at over 60% of troop contributions (see Figure 4), while "many missions with protection responsibilities ... [remained] severely underresourced" (HIPPO, 2015, p. 39),[27] threatening UN credibility both internationally (HIPPO, 2015, p. 24) and in host states (UN_PK14*). Deepening the puzzle, UN officials recognize that multinationalism creates capability-aggregation difficulties ("one of the first challenges of the Force Commander is to bring some cohesion within his force" [UN_PK10*]) that token forces exacerbate:

> There are challenges in relation to small countries. ... There are more people around the table, with opinions and interests, trying to influence decisions. ... The more countries there are ... the more caveats, expectations, and rotation schedules to be managed. There are questions about the complementarity of materiel. ... And there are challenges of national culture. (UN_PK60*)

We argue that understanding token forces from a UN perspective requires moving from a static focus on either legitimacy or capability-aggregation rationales for coalition building to a dynamic understanding of UN coalition builders pursuing both ends while also responding to the growing state demand for token participation documented in Section 3. The first step of

---

[27] Since 2015, personnel shortages have eased due to declining total deployments, but capability gaps persist for specialized contributions and in particular missions (UN, 2021c).

the explanation is the global norm enjoining multinationalism in military interventions, which opened the door to token participation in UN missions by providing UN coalition builders a reason to accept token forces. Beyond this, three dynamics account for both the high incidence and the nature of tokenism in contemporary UN peacekeeping: (1) the UN's limited ability to induce states to move from token to non-token contributions; (2) UN coalition builders' understanding that accommodating token participation demand bolsters support for UN peacekeeping; and (3) UN coalition builders' development of a complex system for channeling token forces to minimize adverse capability-aggregation impacts and, ideally, support peacekeeping effectiveness.

Limited Ability to "Grow" Token Forces

UN officials commonly advocate welcoming token forces as precursors of larger contributions: "We have good examples of countries that started at a very humble level and which step by step developed their capacity" (UN_HQ7). New TCCs

> can deploy individuals as military observers or staff officers. . . . And perhaps you say, after one or two years . . . I can deploy a platoon. . . . That is the way. And this is the reason that you can see there are small units, or small amounts of personnel, for X or Y member state. (UN_HQ4)

Even in the early 1990s, this defense of token forces was not fully convincing, since as noted in Section 2, several early token contributions emerged from previously substantial troop contributors *diminishing* their commitments. Despite prominent examples of states such as China, El Salvador, and Mongolia moving from token to substantial troop contributions, moreover, the credibility of this rationale for tokenism in UN operations further diminished over time. Empirically, as Section 3 shows, token forces are not a significant predictor of subsequent substantial deployments. Some states have remained exclusively token contributors over time. Others continued their original token deployments even as they progressed to contributing substantial contingents to other missions, helping produce the rise in "mixed" portfolios documented in Figure 7. Returning to the earlier examples, both El Salvador and Mongolia maintained their early token contributions (to UNMIL and MONUSCO, respectively) while deploying larger contingents in other missions. Finally, some new token forces are deployed by states that are already large contributors in other missions. For example, France, Ghana, Kenya, and Uruguay joined the UN's newest mission, MINUSCA, with token forces and subsequently maintained that level of commitment. Thus, UN officials acknowledge that progress from token to substantial troop contributions is far from automatic:

> we reached 123 [TCCs], we started with less than 100 . . . many of them with one or two guys . . . and they will remain with these one or two. But . . . when they go to the opening debate of the General Assembly they will say, we participate in this general effort of peacekeeping. (UN_HQ1)

Succinctly, some TCCs "politically want not to provide units, just [individual] personnel" (UN_HQ4).

Yet the very weakness of this explanation for the UN welcoming token forces also holds a reason for persistently high tokenism in UN missions. The UN has limited capacity to induce states to move from token to substantial contributions. A comparison with ISAF is instructive. In 2001–03, when ISAF was confined to Kabul, its coalition builders embraced token forces to cement the operation's international legitimacy and accommodate strong state participation demand within the force's 5,000-troop deployment cap (Coleman, 2017, pp. 350–1). However, following its expansion throughout Afghanistan in 2003–06 and "surge" in response to escalating conflict from 2009, ISAF's troop deployment skyrocketed, reaching over 130,000 by 2010–2011.[28] ISAF coalition builders' attitudes toward token forces evolved correspondingly. They still recognized the legitimacy benefits of a broad coalition – "The point about ISAF is . . . the political power of having 48 nations from across the globe all signed up" (ISAF_6) – and knew that sometimes "a relatively small contribution can have a disproportionately important effect in terms of political legitimacy" (ISAF_22). Thus, they remained eager to welcome even token contributions from states whose presence might mitigate perceptions of ISAF being Western- and USA-dominated and/or anti-Muslim. In all, 14 of the 20 states that joined ISAF between 2003 and 2012 initially participated with under 40 troops.[29] Simultaneously, however, major ISAF contributors demanded greater burden sharing and ISAF coalition builders increasingly prompted token contributors to expand their deployments:

> we have in the past allowed people to sort of join the club by just offering a few staff officers. But more recently, we've said, "Well, if you offer a few staff officers, that's okay, but that's got to be the predecessor to something a bit more substantial." (ISAF_6)

---

[28] ISAF data from NATO placemats, from www.nato.int.
[29] In addition, Jordan and the United Arab Emirates were misleadingly listed as contributing under 40 troops (see below).

On new or aspiring NATO members, this pressure proved highly effective. As the stakes for the Alliance rose ("If we don't succeed in Afghanistan ... we're going to lose all credibility" [ISAF_14]) and the USA excoriated states that "enjoy the benefits of NATO membership but don't want to share the risks and costs" (Shanker, 2011), new and aspiring NATO members recognized that ISAF participation signaled their Alliance commitment: "we would like to act as an ally and show that we are ready to shoulder our burden of membership" (ISAF_21). In 2005–11, Albania, Armenia, Bosnia and Herzegovina, Bulgaria, Czech Republic,[30] Estonia, Georgia, Hungary, Latvia, Lithuania, the Former Yugoslav Republic of Macedonia, Poland, Romania, Slovakia, and Slovenia progressed from token to substantial contributions, all but three deploying over 150 troops. Hungary's defense minister explained bluntly: "This is about NATO, not Afghanistan; what else would we have to do there other than taking responsibility together with our allies?" (Ulrich, 2015, p. 159).[31] The only aspiring NATO members that did not substantially enhance their ISAF participation were Montenegro and Ukraine, which both faced exceptional domestic constraints.

Importantly, token ISAF contributors that were not aspiring NATO members experienced less pressure to expand (ISAF_39) and were less susceptible to such pressure. Austria and Ireland declined direct US invitations to expand their ISAF presence.[32] Switzerland withdrew from ISAF in 2007 (SWI swissinfo.ch, 2007). El Salvador and Tonga recognized that their small deployments (24 and 55 troops) sufficed for their aim of enhancing ties with the USA and the United Kingdom, respectively (Chavez, 2015). Other non-Western and/or Muslim-majority states were keen *not* to signal too close alignment with NATO. Malaysia and Singapore stressed that their token medical personnel did humanitarian work. Jordan and the UAE insisted that their substantial deployments be publicly reported as token contributions (Brown & Ahram, 2015).

In short, in the ISAF case NATO coalition builders credibly cast progress from token to substantial troop contributions as an indicator of commitment to NATO, eliciting a strong response from token contributors wishing to enhance their NATO status but not from other token contributors. For the UN, this suggests two difficulties.

First, with the notable exception of China (Fang et al., 2018; Coleman & Job, 2021), many of the states most interested in enhancing their UN status through peacekeeping contributions have relatively limited military

---

[30] Czech Republic had already contributed a substantial contingent in 2002–2003.

[31] On similar motivations of other states in this group, see Hynek and Marton (2012) and Mattox and Grenier (2015).

[32] Cables from April 8, 2005 and November 27, 2009.

capabilities. United Nations officials note that many small and/or relatively poor countries "are proud to be part of the UN and to be actively part of the UN, and as such they feel they need to give something to the system" (UN_HQ8). For countries emerging from conflict and especially former host countries of UN operations, participating in UN peacekeeping is "a very powerful way of demonstrating their own ability to contribute on the world stage, particularly after an internal conflict" (UN_HQ19). Countries that have faced international opprobrium may also seek a status change: "after the sanctions had been put off, our politicians tried to get in the normal system and one of those things was to contribute to the peacekeeping operations around the world" (UN_PK46). By contrast, powerful Western and other high-income states already benefiting from high UN status as permanent Security Council members and/or as major financial contributors may be less motivated to seek advancement in the hierarchy of UN troop contributors (Coleman, 2020b). Indeed, some view financial contributions as substitutes for troop commitments: "They are not going to submit a significant amount of money and a significant amount of troops" (UN_PK8). Other militarily capable states primarily seek status in organizations other than the UN. Among the 14 NATO members that progressed from token to non-token ISAF contributions by 2010, for example, UN tokenism was high not only during ISAF's peak but also five years later, when NATO's demand for troops had abated but the UN's was at record levels. The number of these states making at least one substantial troop contribution to a large UN mission *shrank* from five in 2010 to two in 2015, while token-only contributors increased from five to eight. In 2020, three made at least one substantial UN contribution and nine deployed only token forces.

Second, the UN's ability to link large troop contributions with status is more tenuous than NATO's. Not only are there few major troop contributors among the UN's most powerful member states, but "[f]or those countries at the top of the UN pecking order, contributing peacekeeping troops seems out of touch with their standing" (Pouliot, 2016, p. 243). Instead, they often make token contributions. This undermines the prestige of making large troop contributions within the UN. It also makes it politically difficult for Secretariat members to criticize token contributions as showing insufficient dedication to the UN. Secretariat members also express a principled commitment to inclusiveness in peacekeeping that makes them reluctant to criticize token contributions:

> the UN obviously wants to give all of its member states who would like to contribute forces to a peacekeeping operation . . . the opportunity to do that.

Because this is an all-inclusive organization. We want everybody to have the opportunity to contribute. (UN_HQ21)

Consequently, "[s]tates that are not among the UN's largest TCC/PCCs rarely feel under significant pressure to contribute more" (Bellamy & Williams, 2012, pp. 7–8).

Accepting Token Forces to Bolster State Support

Why do UN officials welcome even token troop contributions that are unlikely to grow into more substantial ones? The general international legitimacy considerations noted at the beginning of this section provide part of the explanation: "we are always within the Secretariat looking into more universality for peacekeeping" (UN_PK10*). However, UN officials also recognize a more specific political need to reinforce individual member states' support for UN peace operations.

UN officials know that many states both want to "fly their flag in a peacekeeping operation" by making a token contribution (UN_PK6*) and expect to be able to do so: "all the countries that have signed the [UN] Charter . . . can propose and can participate in this peacekeeping operation. You can either participate with military people, army people or military observers" (UN_HQ8). UN coalition builders see such strong state demand for token participation that they typically perceive no need to actively seek token forces: "there's always going to be the onesies, twosies, military observers, staff officers, that sort of thing. So you know you're going to flesh out your force with other flags, it's just inevitable" (UN_HQ21). Put differently, "Individual officers are never a problem. Sometimes the quality of the officers is a problem, but . . . getting them is not a problem" (UN_HQ13). UN officials also note that once states hold particular positions in a mission, including through token forces, they typically expect to keep these posts: "some countries, they think they are entitled to a post, and that is a problem in the UN" (UN_HQ1).

UN coalition builders see it as part of their task to accommodate these demands for (token) participation wherever possible. Principled commitment to inclusiveness in UN peacekeeping plays a role in this: "we are an inclusive organization. And we should respect the intent of member states to want to be involved and get them involved somehow" (UN_HQ12). In addition, however, UN officials recognize that participation bolsters states' support of UN peacekeeping. For example, in mission financing debates, "these [troop] contributing states make the strongest case for why this is the wrong moment for a budget cut" (UNPK_60*). More broadly, "the UN is ready to get every contribution that she can get, because it will be not only a matter of numbers, but a matter of political support, okay, from the side of the country" (UN_HQ8). Welcoming token forces honors the contributing state's material and political support: "one person from any country . . . is an indication of the commitment and awareness of that particular country ... we should be appreciative of that awareness" (UN_PK14*). Rejecting a token contribution offer, meanwhile, risks causing affront:

> if the defense minister in Mongolia says we are going to give you two guys, who is the SRSG in Kinshasa to say, no we don't want them? They may not make a big difference, but they will definitely not be turned away. (UN_PK23*)

UN officials also note that once deployed, token forces help reinforce TCCs' support of UN peacekeeping. "Even if you only have a few troops on the ground, that justifies your Members of Parliament coming to visit" (UN_PK60*), which can be an important tool for building political support (Hannum & Das, 2021). Token forces may also help major financial contributors "be assured about the value for money" in a mission: "whatever report we might be filing ... they are also having means and ways of confirming their own concerns ... if there are issues ... they can confirm through their own, other means. For me, it's an advantage" (UN_PK14*). Finally, welcoming token forces from wealthy states can also have broader material benefits:

> they are members of peacekeeping, so this may raise the interest of the country ... perhaps to fund some initiatives ... perhaps they could be part of triangular partnerships, providing African countries with equipment. I think that [is] part of the purpose as well. (UN_HQ1)

In short, while UN coalition builders rarely actively pursue token forces, they acknowledge states' demand for token participation and perceive a political interest in accommodating this demand: "the political trade-off is that all are welcome" (UN_PK49*).

Adaptation: Channeling Token Troop Contributions

Despite the legitimacy benefits of token forces, the UN's limited capacity to induce token contributors to increase their troop commitments, and political incentives to accept token forces, UN coalition builders never ceased also pursuing capability-aggregation goals. Instead, they have sought ways of accommodating state demand for token participation while also serving, or at least not undermining, mission effectiveness. The SFR developed during the force-generation process (see Section 1) provides one bulwark for capability aggregation: "Coalition builders want as many as possible to be involved, for burden sharing and because it is one UN, we are all equal. But under certain circumstances, [contributions] need to meet Requirements" (UN_HQ17). In addition, however, UN coalition builders have presided over the emergence of co-deployed contingent personnel, staff officers, and military observer positions as distinctive modes of token participation, available under particular conditions to specific sets of states. They have communicated these parameters to (potential) TCCs, but also adapted them further in response to state pressure and initiatives.

Limited and Selective Token Contingent Personnel Contributions

Token contingent personnel contributions must be embedded in a larger contingent since they are too small to operate independently. They can arise in several ways. Two or more states may offer to jointly provide a military unit listed in a mission's SFR, with at least one making a token contribution. A larger TCC already deployed in a mission can allow another state to fill some positions within its contingent. A potential token contributor may also seek UN Secretariat support in finding a larger TCC to co-deploy with (UN_HQ5). While driven by states, all these processes require approval from UN coalition builders. Even in the case of existing TCCs sharing contingent positions, "the UN accepts or not . . . a state can't just say, now I'm bringing someone else along" (UN_PK33).

UN coalition builders have been selective about welcoming this type of token forces because it risks undermining peacekeeping effectiveness by bringing multinational friction into an operational military unit. United Nations officials note that token contingent personnel contributions can be a stepping-stone to larger deployments, not only for new TCCs but also for states that previously made only token staff officer or military observer contributions (UN_HQ7, UN_HQ4). Some also stress a need to respect sovereign states' intentions to enter bilateral co-deployment arrangements (UN_HQ4). Nevertheless, capability-aggregation considerations have led to co-deployed units – including those with token forces – being relatively uncommon in UN operations. Between 2004 and 2014, there were just 41 operational partnerships to deploy formed military units in UN missions, of which 19 involved token forces.[33]

UN coalition builders are selective in the co-deployment arrangements they are willing to support, explicitly discouraging composite units from dissimilar TCCs to minimize the risk of friction:

> My first question . . . is OK, what do you have in common? Besides religion, besides culture, what do you have in common in training? Have you been operating together? How are you going to join a French[-speaking] unit with a Spanish[-speaking] one? That kind of arrangement is the one that we try to avoid. (UN_HQ4)

---

[33] Partnerships identified in (Daniel et al., 2015, pp. 13–14), contribution sizes from UN data at https://peacekeeping.un.org/en/troop-and-police-contributors. Three additional pairings showed contributions just above token level.

UN coalition builders are also selective in where they will accept co-deployed units, typically limiting them to missions with relatively benign operational environments:

> In terms of military efficiency, the more homogeneity at the high level, the better. So if you are in a tough environment, let's say Eastern Congo, a Pakistani brigade or an Indian brigade may be advantageous. . . . It's less important when it's a mission like Cyprus, because . . . the units are not called upon to perform challenging military tasks. (UN_HQ2)

Put differently, in "Cyprus, where frankly it's not the most dangerous of missions . . . you can multinationalize to your heart's content" (UN_HQ21). In all, 12 of the 19 cases of token co-deployed contingent personnel in 2004–14 occurred in relatively safe UN missions in Cyprus, the Golan Heights, and Lebanon.

Selection based on capability-aggregation considerations has historically been rare. Most frequently, token contingent personnel contributions have provided elements of infantry or logistics units (Daniel et al., 2015, pp. 13–14), perhaps modestly easing the larger TCC's deployment strain but not providing specialized capabilities to the mission. In Mali, however, the UN recently welcomed a Dutch-led All Sources Information Fusion Unit and a Norwegian-led rotating C-130 aircraft contribution, both including token forces (Boutellis & Beary, 2020). Both contributions brought niche capabilities to the mission. They were also constituted by highly interoperable NATO militaries and represented a long-sought increase in UN commitments from European states. These factors explain why UN coalition builders welcomed these composite units despite the difficult mission environment. It is not yet clear whether this case will remain exceptional or augurs future opportunities for the UN to selectively welcome token contingent personnel deployments within units that substantially contribute to mission effectiveness.

Strategically Allocated Token Staff Officer Positions

As of April 2021, 2,035 staff officers were deployed across UN peace operations (UN, 2021e). Using some of these positions to accommodate token forces typically presents lower capability-aggregation risks than welcoming token contingent personnel contributions. Differences in training, culture, and language among staff officers may lead to efficiency losses at the individual and team levels, but peacekeeping effectiveness does not depend on headquarters operating as cohesive military units. Thus, "we prefer the units to be from a single country . . . to promote military efficiency . . . Staff officers, on the other hand, it's good for us that they're from all over the world, because it shows that they represent everybody" (UN_HQ11).

However, UN coalition builders face a major constraint on welcoming token staff officer contributions: in UN peacekeeping, "nations fight tooth and nail to have their people in key positions" (UN_HQ21). The United Nations officials know that token senior staff officer contributions are highly attractive to states: "by positioning a very small group of senior officers you can have very much greater influence over the mission" (UN_HQ19). Powerful UN member states often demand this opportunity: "the politically important nations or financially important nations insist on getting at least one senior" appointment (UN_HQ5). Yet states furnishing formed military units to a mission also claim staff officer positions: "this is part of the expectation of many contributors ... they immediately ask to have some staff position, because ... they want to have an eye in the staff" (UN_HQ7). Large TCCs in particular typically demand senior staff officer positions in recognition of their personnel contributions.

To manage these competing demands, UN force generators developed and gradually consolidated a formula. Approximately 70% of staff officer positions are reserved for "member states who actually contribute ... boots on the ground" (UN_HQ5), with the largest TCCs typically claiming senior posts. MONUSCO's Force Chief of Staff position, for example, rotates among Bangladesh, India, and Pakistan. Large TCCs also typically occupy key staff officer positions affecting deployment conditions and personnel policies (UN_PK12). The remaining (roughly) 30% of staff officer positions "are open to other states, and of course certain states have better chances, for political or financial reasons, of getting the important jobs ... it depends on lobbying" (UN_PK43). Thus, token senior staff officer contributions are typically reserved for the most powerful states – and for these states they are not only common but also expected: "our country belongs to the ones who also participate in the financing part of the missions. It's quite normal for [us] to have some people inside the headquarters" (UN_PK5). Thus, in MONUSCO in 2017, the United Kingdom's five deployed peacekeepers included the Senior Military Assistant to the Force Commander and the Chief of Planning; France furnished the Deputy Chief Operations, the head of short-term planning and the Aide de Camp for the (French) Deputy Force Commander; the USA's three peacekeepers included the Deputy Chief of Intelligence; and Canada's eight staff officers included the Deputy Chief of Staff for Operations and the mission's senior liaison officer with the DRC's armed forces. On occasion, UN coalition builders may even use senior posts to persuade powerful states to add their military and political clout to a mission, providing rare instances of UN officials actively seeking token forces:

> [S]ometimes you do need a flag on the table. . . . The national composition is decided at political levels. They are not specific about how many people they want, but about which TCCs they want to see deployed. . . . They may say, we want Americans, so you ring up the Permanent Mission and you say, can you send us a staff officer, these are the positions we have available. (UN_HQ9)

Less powerful states seeking to make token staff officer contributions are usually accommodated in more junior staff officer positions. These positions are less in demand among the mission's TCCs:

> you've . . . got a variety of staff officer positions in operations and personnel and logistics and plans and training and so on that you need to fill. And maybe those nations [contributing formed units] won't necessarily want to fill all of those posts because then you're starting to drain their army. (UN_HQ21)

Lower-ranking staff posts are also of less interest to the UN's most influential member states: "sometimes they don't even use the 30%, and then [the UN] is open to take any qualified officer and nation coming in" (UN_HQ5). This gives UN coalition builders the opportunity to welcome additional token contributors:

> it's good to go to other nations to get those staff officers . . . they may be only small onesies, twosies within the overall picture, but they fill a billet . . . it helps fill your personnel requirements . . . [and] it allows people to contribute. (UN_HQ21)

Some moderately influential token contributors may provide only (mid-level) staff officers. Returning to the MONUSCO example, in 2017, Ireland and Switzerland deployed four and three staff officers, respectively. Other states combine token staff officer and other positions: Burkina Faso, for example, contributed eight MONUSCO military observers and one staff officer in 2017 and Serbia six contingent troops and two staff officers (UN, 2017b). Where vacancies remain or headquarters personnel needs exceed allocated posts, military observers may be redeployed into staff positions (UN_PK7, UN_PK8, UN_PK47).

The extent to which this system also serves capability-aggregation ends – and thus peacekeeping effectiveness – is subject to considerable debate. At the junior staff officer level, token contributors typically complement rather than displace larger TCCs and arguably fill capabilities gaps more effectively than redeploying military observers: "they were sent as military observers, so the function now you want them to perform, as staff officers, it's not what they came here for, so therefore they are not necessarily prepared" (UN_PK14). At more senior levels, the capability-aggregation benefits of token forces are more contested. Western officers often bring excellent skills and operational experience to missions: "the Americans, the Brits, the Canadians . . . they participated in these coalitions of the willing, Afghanistan, Iraq ... So when they come here, they also share in terms of experiences and approaches, in terms of strategic thinking, and planning and execution" (UN_PK14*). Some UN officials see them as vital contributions to missions: "From a force generator's perspective ... I need particular TCCs to bring that experience into the head-quarters, otherwise the headquarters won't run properly" (UN_HQ12).

Yet UN officials also acknowledge that the capability-aggregation benefits of including Western staff officers are not guaranteed: "it doesn't break down in the obvious sense of the guys from the South are bad and the guys from the North are good."[34] Western staff officers may have less UN peacekeeping experience than officers from larger TCCs (UN_PK8), a deficit potentially compounded by rapid (e.g., six-month) rotations. Western states do not always send their best officers on UN deployments: "there are countries which are in a position to provide good officers and ... the officers they provide are some-times of uneven quality ... It depends on the political priorities of the country" (UN_HQ2, also UN_HQ8). Officers from states that do not prioritize UN peacekeeping may also be less motivated: "For some nations, [UN deployment] is good for [officers'] career. This does nothing for my career at all."[35] There are also concerns about token staff officers not fully acknowledging the constraints deployed contingents face:

> When you have these staff officers, coming from the first world, who then are sitting there, who do not necessarily have troops on the ground. Then there is a question mark, can they really be thinking and taking into account the man on the ground? Are they demanding all that they are demanding because it's not their own men? (UN_PK14*)

Illustrating the dynamic, interactive politics surrounding UN token forces, UN force-generation practices for staff officers have continued to evolve. Some changes have targeted specific capability-aggregation concerns applicable to all staff officers but highly relevant for token staff officer contributions. United Nations coalition builders have begun pushing – not always successfully – for longer rotations for key positions. Since 2017, moreover, they have required states to submit three candidates when rotating a senior officer, instead of presenting a single replacement officer (UN_HQ4). The most potent impulse for change, however, has been political contestation of the practice of welcom-ing token senior staff officer contributions. Among the principal challengers are large TCCs, which often resent losing top staff officer positions to powerful token contributors (UN_PK66*). In 2017, the UN's Special Committee on Peacekeeping Operations formally "urge[d] the Secretary-General to ensure

---

[34] Comment not for attribution.   [35] Remark not for attribution.

a fair representation of troop-contributing and police-contributing countries when selecting personnel for such staff positions" (UN, 2017a, §. 390).

UN officials recognize the political weight of this directive. They also acknowledge, sometimes in addition to the capability-aggregation concerns noted earlier, a fundamental political critique: "you can't have a group of countries that is good enough to command the others, and the others are just good enough to follow the orders" (UN_HQ2). More specifically, deploying Western officers in command positions over African, Asian, and Latin American troops raises accusations of neocolonialism that threaten the legitimacy of UN peacekeeping, especially in the global South (Cunliffe, 2013). Yet UN officials also recognize the continued political necessity of welcoming token senior staff officer contributions to ensure the support of major powers:

> they pay for it … and they are then also interested to see what is happening. And also for political reasons … Security Council members, Canada, Germany and other nations might be interested to have some people there to see what is going on … to have a good feeling that all the effort being put in by the UN is being applied correctly. (UN_HQ5)

Formally, the UN has thus shifted away from the practice of "flagging" posts to particular countries: "most of the senior positions … now, since 2017, they are becoming competitive. We invite four to five member states to provide a candidate, and then we … [seek] to deploy the most suitable candidate for the post" (UN_HQ4). It remains to be seen how significant this shift will be in practice, since powerful states can resist efforts to open senior officer posts they occupy to competitive bids from other states: "you can start geopolitical engagement and then that decision can be changed. This is a political organization."[36]

Permissive Welcome to Token Military Observer (UNMO) Contributions

UN officials have long recognized that "the composition of the UNMOs is one of the best ways, let's say, to give a demonstration of the universality of peacekeeping" (UN_PK10). UNMOs work in small teams that are separate from the mission's military contingents to "observe and monitor the security and humanitarian situation" in their area of responsibility, reporting up their chain of command to mission headquarters (UNDPKO & UNDFS, 2017, p. 3). Two factors make UNMOs an excellent mechanism for welcoming token forces into UN peace operations.

---

[36] Comment not for attribution.

First, multinationalism is considered essential to UNMO teams, undergirding rather than undermining their operational effectiveness. Under the "rainbow concept," each UNMO team member must deploy from a different country. Any resulting interpersonal challenges are understood to be outweighed by operational benefits (UN_PK63), including impartial reporting – "The rainbow concept, this is how you get objectivity, neutrality" (UN_PK28) – and mission credibility: "the UN actually tries to get ... member states involved in the observers, to really show ... the UN open accountability, through multiple nations coming and not having one nation being dominating and doing the observing" (UN_HQ5). Multinationalism may also improve team productivity: "If there is less diversity, sometimes that pushes people to be lazy" (UN_PK63). Token forces are not strictly necessary for achieving multinational teams, since a handful of large UNMO contributors distributing their personnel across team sites could produce the same effect. However, token UNMO contributions are easily integrated: "military observers, to have them in small numbers from one particular country, that's not really a problem ... They don't operate as a group. So the size is, in a way, irrelevant" (UN_HQ2).

Second, the barriers to deploying UNMOs are relatively low. While they require some specialized training, "the skillset for a military observer is, I would say, standard military. They know how the military works, they know how to write reports, they know [how] to observe something" (UN_HQ5). Consequently, "all countries, even the poorest one[s], can well train a couple of observers" (UN_HQ8). Once deployed, moreover, UNMOs receive an allowance to cover their living expenses, relieving TCCs of the need to supply logistic support and often providing a financial benefit to deployed personnel (Coleman, 2013, pp. 61–2). Finally, for much of the 2000s and 2010s, UNMO positions were relatively available. United Nations demand was high as peace operations expanded, and while existing TCCs often sought UNMO positions for their officers, powerful states focused primarily on securing staff officer positions: "we used to have a MilOb, but we decided the position wasn't influential enough ... Because if you're already in the [staff officer] club, why would you bother with the MilOb?" (UN_PK15). Consequently, "when it comes to observers, it's more open, the chances of deploying observers even if you have no large contingent are absolutely existent" (UN_HQ17).

For UN coalition builders, therefore, UNMOs have long presented both a means of broadening UN peacekeeping coalitions – "that's the kind of UN model that buys it the legitimacy" (UN_PK54) – and an opportunity to accommodate state demand for (token) participation without undermining peacekeeping effectiveness. Indeed they have actively guided states to this option: "You want to participate? We suggest you prepare some guys to be military observers ... OK, let's find a way of giving you some observer posts" (UN_HQ1). United Nations officials not only note that token UNMO contributions can be a "first step" into UN peacekeeping for new TCCs (UN_HQ5) but may also recommend them as such: "you don't have to run if you've never walked" (UN_HQ4). As noted earlier, however, they also recognize that many contributions remain at token levels.

As with staff officers, the practice of welcoming token UNMOs emerged informally. Once established, however, it has proved remarkably resilient. There are long-standing debates about the operational utility of UNMOs – "The issue of military observers has been a big debate in UN missions for a long time" (UN_PK66*) – raising questions about the capability-aggregation benefits of welcoming any UNMO contributions, including token ones. The UN warned in 2002 that "too many UNMOs arrive in a mission area incapable of effectively executing their tasks" (UN, 2002, p. iii). The UN's Office of Military Affairs has since increased its capacity to verify the qualifications of nominated officers (UN_HQ5), but the concern persists: "Some countries do not send the right representative to a UN operation" (UN_PK63). Another long-standing critique is that UNMOs are not necessarily trained to analyze their observations – "they just pick up information and they send it up the chain of command" (UN_PK31*) – or able to place observations in a larger strategic context: they "are often looking down the 'drinking straw' at their own little area" (UN_PK47) and thus "much more involved in tactical overview of situation[s] than ... operational overview" (UN_PK5).

The debate about UNMOs' utility gained new urgency as the UN shifted toward more robust enforcement and stabilization operations in the 2010s (Karlsrud, 2018), since

> [a] deteriorating or fragile security environment can hinder UNMO freedom of movement, preventing them from effectively performing their tasks ... UNMO are vulnerable to harassment, attack and hostage taking. They represent a soft target for belligerents. ... Unstable security situations do not permit UNMO to perform their functions effectively and independently. (UNDPKO & UNDFS, 2017, pp. 3, 7–8)

Thus, one MONUSCO official commented, "can you really send them into [high-conflict] areas like Beni ... and be comfortable and go to bed, and sleep?" (UN_PK14*) – especially given UNMOs' reduced operational benefits in "red" (i.e., dangerous) zones: "why I must have a military observer in a red zone, and ... he must be under [protective military] escort? I might as well send that escort, they will bring me the same information" (UN_PK14*). United Nations Military Observers can be redeployed to relative "islands of stability" where unarmed deployment remains feasible (UN_HQ5), but that also removes them from the main areas of interest to the mission (UN_PK47). Moreover, missions with enforcement mandates typically have alternative sources of information: "if I plan for a military offensive operation, I will get information from the U2 [intelligence branch], I will get information from ISR [intelligence, surveillance, and reconnaissance] . . . I will take some of the information from the MilObs, but it's very low" (UN_PK55; also UN_PK1). In short, while token forces pose no risk of undermining the operational effectiveness of UNMO teams, the overall contribution of UNMOs to mission effectiveness has come under increasing doubt.

Reflecting these dynamics, the average number of UNMOs per UN mission decreased from 124 January 2010 to 105 in January 2017. It then plummeted as UN peacekeeping contracted amid waning political and financial support from major powers (Coleman, 2020b), reaching 52 UNMOs per mission in January 2021 (UN, 2021f). Proportionally, UNMOs accounted for 2.78% of UN military peacekeepers in 2010, 1.75% in 2017, and 1.59% in 2021. Departing from post-Cold War practice, MINUSMA was launched without UNMOs in 2013 because of the mission's difficult operational environment; it gained a small (40-strong) UNMO component in 2015, but this was eliminated following a 2019 strategic review (UN, 2020c).

Even in severe contractions, however, UN coalition builders protected token troop contributors. In MONUSCO, for example, UNMO deployments declined by 65% (from 479 to 167) between 2016 and 2021, compared to a 19% decline in the mission's overall military personnel (UN, 2016, 2021f). Yet these reductions were overwhelmingly absorbed by the mission's larger TCCs, 13 of which became token UNMO contributors in the process. Of the 14 states making token UNMO contributions in January 2016, only two (Sri Lanka and Yemen) left MONUSCO, Sweden became a police contributor only and Belgium a token staff officer only contributor. With Bhutan and Brazil joining, the net number of token UNMO contributors *rose* to 25, helping MONUSCO's military coalition shrink by only one state (from 50 to 49), despite its personnel reductions. A senior MONUSCO officer explained the rationale in 2017:

> it's the United Nations. So I want those flags . . . If then somebody is sending 16 military observers, the other person is sending two. Really, you just want to send home these two? Really? And I say no, please just take two away from the 16, they still have 14. (UN_PK14*)

A similar logic prevails at UN Headquarters: when preparing downsizing options, planners

> try to keep the representation and decrease the numbers. Perhaps you were providing 10, 50% is five, but the other who was providing one, they continue

providing one and you instead of five are going to provide four. . . . The first option is, OK, we are keeping the number of TCCs and we reduce the number proportionally, and we fine-tune on those that are providing a small number to keep the representation. (UN_HQ4)

This approach has largely prevailed, despite protests from bigger contributors having to absorb disproportionate reductions (UN_HQ4). Even in the extreme case of MINUSMA eliminating its UNMO component, token participation was protected. All 40 UNMO positions were converted to staff officer posts (UN Secretary-General, 2020a, §. 133), and six of the seven states whose token contributions included UNMOs in August 2019 remained token contributors (typically with slightly more staff officers) in April 2021. The seventh, Lithuania, crossed the threshold to a more substantial contribution of 45 troops.

In short, despite increasing doubts about UNMOs' operational utility UN coalition builders have protected token UNMO contributions wherever possible, testifying not only to states' eagerness to provide these contributions but also to coalition builders' recognition of the political value of welcoming them.

Conclusion

International legitimacy considerations help explain UN coalition builders' willingness to welcome large numbers of token forces into UN operations, but they only provide the starting point of the explanation. United Nations coalition builders rarely see a need to actively solicit token forces because they understand broad coalitions as reinforcing UN operations' already high international legitimacy rather than remedying significant legitimacy deficits. They do, however, recognize a political need to accommodate states' demand for token participation in order to bolster support for UN peacekeeping and their limited leverage to induce token contributors to progress to more substantial contributions. Simultaneously, UN officials are keenly aware that the capability-aggregation dimension of coalitions remains central to peacekeeping effectiveness. Consequently, UN coalition builders gradually identified and consolidated three distinct mechanisms for channeling token contributions that mitigate adverse capability-aggregation effects: limited and selective contingent troop co-deployment, strategically allocated staff officer positions, and permissive allocation of UNMO positions. They continue to refine these mechanisms in response to operational demands and member state contestation.

5 Conclusion

United Nations peacekeeping is in turmoil (Boutellis, 2020; Williams, 2020; Coleman & Job, 2021; Coleman & Williams, 2021). In addition to some relatively successful missions ending, waning state support and persistent demands for cost reductions have led to multiple rounds of downsizing in ongoing missions while growing divisions within the Security Council have impeded the creation of any major new mission since 2014. One result has been a sharp decline in UN troop deployments: between April 2016 and April 2021, the number of military UN peacekeepers shrank by 22.5%, from 91,651 to 71,028 (UN, 2021d).

The phenomenon of token forces, however, remains vibrant. In April 2021, 48 of the UN's 118 troop contributors deployed fewer than 40 troops each, often spread over several missions. At the other end of the troop contributors' spectrum, each of the five largest TCCs (Bangladesh, Ethiopia, India, Nepal, and Rwanda) furnished over 4,500 troops – but also made at least one token troop contribution (UN, 2021d). UNFICYP, which featured early instances of token forces (see Section 2), provides a striking example of their continued vibrancy. The mission recently gained three new token troop contributors: Pakistan joined with one staff officer in September 2018, India deployed one staff officer in April 2019, and Russia contributed its first two UNFICYP staff officers in December 2019.[37] As of April 2021, these states contributed three, one, and four staff officers, respectively. These contributions did not provide scarce niche capabilities: among the posts filled was a Visits and Protocol Officer (Russia) and a Military Public Information Officer (Pakistan) (UNFICYP, 2019, p. 23, 2021). UNFICYP was not short of personnel: total mission troop requirements shrank from 889 in 2019 to 796 in 2020 and existing major TCCs (Argentina, Slovakia, and the United Kingdom) relinquished staff officer positions when the new token contributors joined. The new token contributions also did not introduce new TCCs to UN peacekeeping: all three states already had extensive UN peacekeeping experience; India and Pakistan have long been top UN TCCs. Thus neither immediate nor longer-term capability-aggregation consideration satisfactorily explain the addition of three new token contributors – but neither do legitimacy concerns: UNFICYP is a long-established, peaceful mission deployed with host state consent and is facing no significant international legitimacy challenges.

Our explanation of token forces in UN peace operations can account for the continued vibrancy of tokenism because it adds an interactive and path-dependent dimension to existing arguments about the impact of, and tension between, capability-aggregation and legitimation rationales for contemporary coalition building. We have conceptualized token forces as rooted in

---

[37] Russia deployed three to seven police officers to UNFICYP from 2016 onwards. India has long contributed small numbers of UNFICYP police.

international legitimacy considerations but also driven by a dynamic interplay between two sets of actors: troop contributors, who are often motivated to deploy token forces and have learned to expect to be able to do so, and UN coalition builders, who respond to international legitimacy considerations and member states' participation demands, have limited leverage to persuade states to grow their troop contributions, and have developed institutional mechanisms for accommodating token forces without excessively undermining the peacekeeping coalition's military effectiveness. Those mechanisms, in turn, shape both the expectations of states and UN officials' force-generation practices.

In this concluding section, we summarize our main empirical findings and then discuss our conceptual contributions and possible extensions of our argument.

Summary of Empirical Findings

Token forces have become ubiquitous in large UN peace operations. In Section 2 we documented that token forces were rare during the Cold War and in the early 1990s, became more common in the mid-1990s, and skyrocketed both in number and as a proportion of all UN troop contributions in the early 2000s. They then plateaued, largely maintaining their share of troop contributions even as UN peacekeeping contracted from 2015 onward. Tokenism occurs in all major UN peace operations. In older missions, token forces were gradually incorporated in the 1990s and 2000s. Missions created from the 2000s onward show high levels of tokenism from inception. Tokenism is also ubiquitous across TCCs: democracies and autocracies, rich and poor countries, and TCCs with large and small armed forces all at least occasionally make token troop contributions. Indeed, over our 29-year period of observation, just four of the UN's 151 troop contributors never made a token contribution – and three of them ceased participating in major UN peace operations in the 2000s.

Section 3 examined this explosion of tokenism from the perspective of TCCs. States unwilling or unable to make a substantial troop contribution to a UN peace operation may wish to deploy token forces because of the prestige associated with participating in highly legitimate UN peace operations, the low cost of token participation, and the benefits of particular token contribution types: operational influence (staff officers), information (military observers), and improved bilateral relations and interoperability (co-deployed contingent troops). Yet states can only deploy to a UN operation if UN coalition builders accept their contribution. A state's decision to offer token forces therefore depends not only on its perceived national interest but also on its belief that token participation is a realistic option in UN peacekeeping. States can learn this through their own experience, if they negotiate with UN coalition builders and reach agreement on a token troop contribution. However, they can also observe tokenism in other states, especially those similar to them in politically relevant ways. Section 3 presents evidence of this type of learning, documenting how tokenism diffuses among neighboring states over time.

We take up the UN's perspective of this interactive story in Section 4. Drawing on extensive interviews, we show that UN officials value the legitimacy broad coalitions provide. However, since UN operations enjoy considerable international legitimacy but have long been dogged by personnel shortfalls, UN coalition builders have no reason to prioritize legitimacy over capability aggregation. Their willingness to welcome such high rates of token participation thus reflects three additional dynamics. First, UN coalition builders have limited leverage to persuade token contributors to progress to substantial troop contributions, a weakness illuminated in contrast to NATO's influence over new and aspiring Alliance members. Second, UN officials also cannot easily reject token forces, not only because they have a principled commitment to inclusiveness in peacekeeping but also because accommodating state participation expectations bolsters political support for UN peace operations. Third, the UN has gradually evolved institutional mechanisms enabling it to respond to state demand for token participation while minimizing adverse effects on capability aggregation. Officials selectively channel prospective token contributors into three contribution types: co-deployed contingent troops (for compatible/interoperable partners, largely in safer missions), staff officers (with senior positions allocated to the most powerful states), and military observers (broadly allocated among TCCs).

Contributions and Extensions

This Element presents the first systematic analysis of the evolution and pattern of token forces as a major form of participation in UN peacekeeping. In highlighting token contributions as a distinctive and frequently chosen alternative to both substantial deployments and nonparticipation in a UN mission, we add nuance to theories of TCC motivations for contributing peacekeepers and highlight a neglected dimension of UN force generation and composition. Our original UNTFD allows for further investigation of patterns of tokenism by particular states or in particular missions, including as mandated tasks change (Di Salvatore et al., 2022). The UNTFD also provides a foundation for studying the further evolution of tokenism – or particular forms of tokenism, such as military observer contributions – through the current contraction and possible reinvention of UN peacekeeping (Coleman, 2020a; Coleman & Job, 2021; Coleman & Williams, 2021). In addition, our study makes three broader conceptual contributions that invite further empirical investigations.

UN Force-Generation and Peacekeeping Effectiveness

With respect to UN peacekeeping, we illuminate a major aspect of force generation that has important implications for peacekeeping effectiveness but is not driven by (military) effectiveness considerations.

There is an extensive literature linking peacekeeping effectiveness to the number, quality and composition of troops (and police) in UN missions (e.g., Hultman et al., 2013; Haass & Ansorg, 2018; Bove et al., 2020). Yet these factors are overwhelmingly driven by large troop contributions that are typically only made by a small subset of a mission's TCCs.

Token forces are orthogonal to peacekeeping effectiveness. They did not arise because they were required to implement mission mandates. They do not generate sufficient troops to remedy the personnel shortfalls UN missions have long suffered. With the possible and contested exception of senior staff officers from powerful Western states, they rarely provide niche capabilities significantly expanding a mission's military capacities beyond what major TCCs can provide. Instead, token forces arose because the global norm of multinationalism in military interventions gave UN coalition builders an incentive to accept token contributions, and states have found this mode of participation in UN missions remarkably attractive.

Token forces nevertheless impact peacekeeping effectiveness. They can have adverse repercussions, bringing multinational tensions into operational military units (for co-deployed contingent personnel), increasing the number of states seeking to shape mission policies and multiplying the challenges of coalition management for UN officials. Moreover, personnel shortfalls may be exacerbated as states capable of deploying large contingents instead choose token participation. However, the impact of token forces on peacekeeping effectiveness is neither unidirectional nor static. United Nations has evolved a sophisticated system for managing token forces and maximizing their operational benefit. Token contingent troop contributions are limited to the most auspicious cases, with interoperable partners and benign mission conditions – or, most recently, exceptional capability provision. Senior staff officer positions are allocated only to the most powerful states, which also have highly capable officers, with (increasingly) policies to ensure the quality of deployed officers and allow competitive challenges. Military observers may not significantly enhance UN mission's capabilities in many conflict environments, but these positions allow a broader accommodation of token contributors without undermining military effectiveness. Moreover, token forces can enhance peacekeeping effectiveness in nonmilitary ways, notably by building the political support a mission can muster for its initiatives.

These impacts notwithstanding, exploring token forces serves as a reminder that while UN coalitions are central to peacekeeping effectiveness they are not solely built for capability aggregation. United Nations force generation is deeply political, both from the point of view of TCCs (whose interests extend, often in multiple ways, beyond the success of the mission to which they are contributing) and from the perspective of UN coalition builders managing relationships with member states and seeking to bolster support for UN peacekeeping. To focus solely on capability aggregation leaves a majority of contemporary troop contributions to UN missions fundamentally underexplained.

Interactive Coalition Building

We add a path-dependent, interactive, and potentially institutionalized dimension to the literature on multinational military coalition building. This approach suggests a framework not only for systematic comparison of token forces across coalition types but also for analyzing progress and bottlenecks toward other coalition building objectives.

Instead of focusing on whether (or when) coalition builders prioritize capability aggregation or legitimacy, our investigation of token forces envisions coalition builders as seeking to optimize both goals in a dynamic interaction with (potential) TCCs that responds to existing state expectations and institutional mechanisms and also shapes these over time. Coalition builders weigh the capability and legitimation needs of their operation but also consider whether states are offering (or demanding) to participate and, if so, how they intend to participate. Potential TCCs weigh their national interests with regard to a particular intervention, but how they seek to pursue those interests depends significantly on their beliefs about the kinds of participation the coalition builder will accept. Both sets of actors' calculations reflect their past experience, observation of others' behavior, and, if the intervention is launched through an international organization, their understanding of that organization's force-generation mechanisms and practices. In turn, these actors' coalition building and deployment decisions shape state expectations as well as national and (where relevant) institutional coalition building practices for subsequent interventions.

This approach provides a framework for a systematic empirical comparison of how token forces have evolved across different coalition types. Section 4 illustrated the utility of such comparisons by noting differential pressures to grow token forces in NATO and the UN. While a full comparative exploration is beyond the scope of this volume, we identify four factors as likely to produce systematic differences in tokenism across coalition types.

First, the extent to which coalition builders seek broad participation to bolster their operation's legitimacy shapes their demand for token forces. This demand is likely highest when operations face significant international legitimacy challenges, such as deploying without a UN mandate or accusations of bias. Demand will be lower when coalition builders are confident in their operation's international legitimacy and/or prioritize legitimacy audiences whose assessments are unlikely to be swayed by token forces, such as host communities demanding effective protection (Coleman, 2017).

Second, an operation's international legitimacy also shapes the supply of token forces. Here the effect on tokenism is in the opposite direction. Highly legitimate operations attract token forces, as states unwilling to deploy larger contingents nevertheless seek the prestige of participation. For controversial operations, states not sufficiently committed to deploy large contingents are more likely to prefer not participating to risking international opprobrium by deploying token forces. This analysis suggests two fundamental types of tokenism in peace operations: supply-driven tokenism, reflecting TCC eagerness to participate, and demand-driven tokenism, arising from coalition builders' active recruitment efforts. United Nations peace operations exemplify the former, MNF-I in Iraq the latter.

Third, tokenism levels depend on the leverage coalition builders can mobilize to persuade token contributors to increase their troop deployments. Section 4 suggested that for interventions launched through an international organization, that leverage depends on a TCC's interest in enhancing its status in the organization and on coalition builders' ability to credibly link larger contributions and status. For other interventions, bilateral status-seeking with the lead state and that state's ability to link larger troop commitments to closer bilateral relations play equivalent roles.

The fourth factor comprises the mechanisms and practices for accommodating token forces that are available to coalition builders and known by potential TCCs. We have shown that in the UN context, these are co-deployed contingent troops, staff officers, and military observers. NATO does not deploy military observers, but its emphasis on interoperability enhancements may offer greater co-deployment opportunities. Empirically, both ISAF and the multinational force in Iraq appear to have accommodated smaller troop contributions in static defense positions (ISAF_6, ISAF_2, ISAF_30). Other coalitions and coalition types (e.g., Africa Union-led coalitions) may evolve different practices for welcoming token forces.

This framework can be adapted beyond token forces to illuminate other contemporary coalition building dynamics. For example, multiple international actors including the UN, NATO, the European Union, the African Union and the Organization for Security and Co-operation in Europe have declared a goal of increasing the number of uniformed women deployed in their peace operations (Olsson et al., 2015; African Union, 2020). Our framework highlights that the success of such initiatives depends not only on how strong this demand for women peacekeepers is but also on TCCs' willingness to deploy more women, coalition builders' leverage over TCCs, and the available mechanisms for women's deployment. Consequently, institutional actors committed to deploying more women should not only request more female troops from TCCs but also attempt to shape the latter three factors. The UN, for example, has sought to: (1) increase TCCs' willingness to deploy uniformed women through the Elsie Initiative Fund for Uniformed Women in Peace Operations;[38] (2) gain leverage by committing to reallocate highly attractive staff officer and military observer positions if TCCs do not meet targets of women's representation (UN, 2019); and (3) develop institutional innovations to promote the deployment of women peacekeepers, such as amending the "rainbow concept" for military observer teams to allow two women of the same nationality to deploy together and developing the concept of "mixed engagement teams" including both women and men within military contingents (UNSC, 2020, p. 4). Whether these efforts prove effective will depend on states' reactions, including their decisions on whether to apply for Elsie Fund resources and whether they (successfully) challenge deployment reductions based on insufficient female peacekeepers (UN_HQ1). The importance of leverage is illustrated by the fact that by August 2020 gender targets were met for staff officers and military observers (which are attractive to states and for which the UN can more easily find alternative TCCs) whereas contingents lagged considerably behind their significantly lower targets (UN Secretary-General, 2020b, p. 10).

IOs, Adaptation and the Unintended Consequences of Norms

Our broadest conceptual contribution is to highlight the scope for global norms and norm-driven institutional innovations to produce unintended but durable behavior over time, as strategic international actors seek new ways to pursue their interests or learn about such opportunities by observing others' behavior. The global norm of multinationalism in international interventions is at best silent on token forces. Nevertheless, it has ultimately shaped coalition builders' incentives to accept token forces, TCCs' expectations of being able to deploy

---

[38] See this UNDP factsheet for details: http://mptf.undp.org/factsheet/fund/EIF00.

them, and the mechanisms by which the UN accommodates token forces. The process recalls historical institutionalist analyses of unintended consequences in Comparative Politics (Merton, 1936; Hall & Taylor, 1996; Thelen, 2004), which we suggest hold important lessons for scholars of international organizations, who thus far have been more focused on unintended consequences of norm implementation rather than of norm and institution creation.[39]

Further empirical investigation is warranted to fully investigate similar dynamics in other international cases. Nevertheless, we can identify apparently promising examples. Graham and Serdaru (2020, p. 682) have suggested that changes to UN funding rules originally intended to allow programmatic agencies to expand their activities have also unintentionally allowed major funders to exert increased influence via earmarked financial contributions. The WTO's dispute settlement mechanism (DSM) provides another potential illustration. The DSM requires cases to go through consultations before escalating to adjudication, reflecting the WTO's commitment to "settle disputes through consultations if possible" (WTO, 2020) and member preferences for early settlement (Busch & Reinhardt, 2006). To enhance the DSM's internal transparency and reduce its participation deficit, especially among new and developing-country members (Li, 2012), the WTO allows states not directly engaged in a dispute to join as third parties, which enables them to observe dispute proceedings and/or present their views. The initial normative purpose of this mechanism has been overshadowed, however, as both rich and poor countries have over time learned to take advantage of third-party participation strategically to pursue their own agendas – for example, to warn the court of potential adverse implications of its jurisprudence. Consequently, the DSM saw significant increases in the number of third parties, which produced further unintended consequences (Pelc, 2017) including a reduced likelihood of early settlement (Johns & Pelc, 2018) and compliance with rulings (Kucik & Peritz, 2021). Thus, broader participation in the form of third parties may have inadvertently created the greatest obstacle to the DSM's core aim of resolving trade disputes.

In short, in addition to systematically exploring the emergence of the most popular form of military participation in UN peace operations, this Element shines conceptual light on the multiple purposes of UN force generation and broader dynamics of contemporary military coalition building. It also highlights the potential for international normative and institutional innovations to produce unintended but durable new forms of behavior, as strategic international actors learn to exploit the new opportunities these innovations offer to pursue existing interests in novel ways.

---

[39] For example, on peacekeeping, see Jennings (2010) and Hunt (2017).

Abbreviations

DPO	Department of Peace Operations
DRC	Democratic Republic of Congo
DSM	dispute settlement mechanism
IPI	International Peace Institute
IR	International Relations
ISAF	International Security Assistance Force
MINUSCA	UN Multidimensional Integrated Stabilization Mission in the Central African Republic
MINUSMA	UN Multidimensional Integrated Stabilization Mission in Mali
MINUSTAH	UN Stabilization Mission in Haiti
MNF-I	Multi-National Force – Iraq
MONUA	UN Observer Mission in Angola
MONUC	UN Organization Stabilization Mission in the Congo
MONUSCO	UN Organization Stabilization Mission in the Democratic Republic of the Congo
NATO	North Atlantic Treaty Organization
OMA	Office of Military Affairs
ONUC	UN Operation in the Congo
PCC	police-contributing country
PCRS	Peacekeeping Capabilities Readiness System
PKO	peacekeeping operation
SRSG	Special Representative of the Secretary-General
TCC	troop-contributing country
UAE	United Arab Emirates
UN	United Nations
UNAMA	UN Assistance Mission in Afghanistan
UNAMID	African Union-UN Hybrid Operation in Darfur
UNAMSIL	UN Mission in Sierra Leone
UNDOF	UN Disengagement Observer Force
UNDPKO	UN Department of Peacekeeping Operations
UNEF	UN Emergency Force
UNFICYP	UN Peacekeeping Force in Cyprus
UNIFIL	UN Interim Force in Lebanon
UNMEE	UN Mission in Ethiopia and Eritrea
UNMIL	UN Mission in Liberia

UNMISS	UN Mission in South Sudan
UNMO	UN military observer
UNOCI	UN Operation in Côte d'Ivoire
UNOSOM	UN Operation in Somalia
UNPREDEP	UN Preventive Deployment Force
UNPROFOR	UN Protection Force
UNSC	UN Security Council
UNTFD	UN Token Forces Dataset
UNTSO	UN Truce Supervision Organization
WDI	World Development Indicators
WTO	World Trade Organization

Appendix

Table A1 UN peacekeeping missions in the UNTFD

Mission	Host country	Start	End	Troops	TCCs	Tokenism
MINURCA	Central African Republic	1998	1999	1,137	14	0.09
MINURCAT	Chad	2009	2010	1,590	40	0.73
MINUSCA	Central African Republic	2014	2018*	9,415	49	0.59
MINUSMA	Mali	2013	2018*	9,695	48	0.60
MINUSTAH	Haiti	2004	2017	5,810	47	0.37
MONUA	Angola	1997	1997	1,129	29	0.51
MONUC	DR Congo	2001	2010	11,174	53	0.44
MONUSCO	DR Congo	2010	2018*	17,279	56	0.49
ONUB	Burundi	2004	2006	4,357	44	0.81
ONUCI	Côte d'Ivoire	2005	2006	6,487	50	0.74
ONUMOZ	Mozambique	1993	1994	5,327	28	0.17
UNAMID	Sudan	2008	2018*	13,016	48	0.58
UNAMIR	Rwanda	1994	1996	3,031	21	0.38
UNAMSIL	Sierra Leone	1999	2005	9,737	36	0.50
UNAVEM	Angola	1995	1997	2,763	34	0.33
UNCRO	Croatia	1995	1995	8,806	34	0.34
UNDOF	Syrian Arab Republic	1990*	2014†	1,038	5	0.26

Table A1 (cont.)

Mission	Host country	Start	End	Troops	TCCs	Tokenism
UNFICYP	Cyprus	1990*	2004[†]	1,044	9	0.54
UNIFIL	Lebanon	1990*	2018*	9,569	21	0.21
UNISFA	Sudan	2011	2018*	3,932	31	0.97
UNMEE	Eritrea	2001	2007	2,643	44	0.83
UNMIH	Haiti	1995	1996	3,658	11	0.49
UNMIL	Liberia	2003	2016	8,705	57	0.76
UNMIS	Sudan	2005	2011	8,006	66	0.59
UNMISET	Timor-Leste	2002	2004	2,582	42	0.63
UNMISS	South Sudan	2011	2018*	9,521	64	0.80
UNOCI	Côte d'Ivoire	2004	2017	6,606	49	0.77
UNOSOM	Somalia	1993	1994	15,259	23	0.23
UNOSOM II	Somalia	1994	1995	13,330	17	0.42
UNPROFOR	Croatia	1992	1996	20,340	34	0.35
UNSMIH	Haiti	1996	1997	1,262	10	0.47
UNTAC	Cambodia	1992	1993	11,536	40	0.32
UNTAES	Croatia	1996	1997	2,742	29	0.74
UNTAET	Timor-Leste	2000	2002	5,925	48	0.50
UNTMIH	Haiti	1997	1997	1,064	12	0.00

Note: Start and end years denoted by * are not the actual start and end times of the missions due to the time coverage of the IPI dataset from 1990 to 2018. End year denoted by [†] indicates that the missions are still active in 2018 but the troops have dropped below 1,000. Troops, TCCs, and tokenism are averaged across the duration of each mission. Troops do not include military observers. ONUCI and UNOCI are variations of the UN mission in Côte d'Ivoire listed as separate missions in the original IPI dataset.

Table A2 Determinants of mode of participation in UN peacekeeping operations (using regional diffusion measures)

Variable	Token force	Mixed	Non-token force
Regional token force participation	1.138	1.734*	−1.185
	(0.782)	(0.800)	(0.905)
Regional mixed participation	−0.795	1.122	−1.622*
	(0.659)	(0.642)	(0.654)
Armed forces personnel (logged)	−0.0712	−0.165	−0.0351
	(0.103)	(0.111)	(0.113)
Population (logged)	0.328**	0.639**	0.450**
	(0.120)	(0.133)	(0.133)
GDP per capita (logged)	0.204*	0.0736	0.0850
	(0.0804)	(0.0719)	(0.0728)
Polity score	0.0477**	0.0637**	0.0673**
	(0.0179)	(0.0194)	(0.0169)
Host	−1.381**	−2.183**	−0.812
	(0.369)	(0.542)	(0.624)
Casualty	0.0913	0.703	0.723
	(0.433)	(0.428)	(0.432)
Ongoing mission, global	−0.154	−0.205**	−0.207**
	(0.0873)	(0.0660)	(0.0774)
Ongoing mission, regional	0.112*	0.119*	0.151*
	(0.0473)	(0.0517)	(0.0630)
Mission hosts polity scores	−0.369**	−0.681**	−0.537**
	(0.107)	(0.104)	(0.123)
Mission hosts population (logged)	−0.0516	−0.323*	−0.288
	(0.168)	(0.126)	(0.194)
Mission hosts GDP per capita (logged)	−2.198**	−2.058**	−1.688**
	(0.348)	(0.356)	(0.353)
Token force contribution $(t-1)$	4.542**	3.433**	0.791
	(0.215)	(0.268)	(0.608)
Mixed contribution $(t-1)$	3.013**	6.174**	3.873**
	(0.251)	(0.303)	(0.312)
Non-token contribution $(t-1)$	1.046*	4.156**	4.571**
	(0.482)	(0.281)	(0.271)
Constant	9.701*	8.993*	9.042*
	(4.547)	(4.240)	(4.578)
Observations	3,602	3,602	3,602

Table A2 (cont.)

Variable	Token force	Mixed	Non-token force
Pseudo R-squared	0.543	0.543	0.543
Chi squared	3,696	3,696	3,696
Log likelihood	−2,050	−2,050	−2,050

Note: Robust standard errors clustered by country in parentheses. ** $p < 0.01$, * $p < 0.05$

Table A3 Determinants of mode of participation in UN peacekeeping operations (with diffusion measures lagged by one year)

Variable	Token force	Mixed	Non-token force
Neighbor token force participation (t–1)	2.649**	0.0302	−1.098
	(0.589)	(0.479)	(0.640)
Neighbor mixed participation ($t - 1$)	0.323	1.497**	0.241
	(0.566)	(0.383)	(0.366)
Armed forces personnel (logged)	−0.204	−0.229	−0.158
	(0.181)	(0.192)	(0.168)
Population (logged)	0.539**	0.946**	0.730**
	(0.205)	(0.225)	(0.204)
GDP per capita (logged)	0.355**	0.184	0.195
	(0.130)	(0.116)	(0.105)
Polity score	0.0729**	0.114**	0.0906**
	(0.0280)	(0.0302)	(0.0244)
Host	−2.160**	−3.010**	−1.080*
	(0.555)	(0.749)	(0.548)
Casualty	0.644	1.507*	1.498*
	(0.574)	(0.608)	(0.616)
Ongoing mission, global	−0.0651	0.0592	−0.0515
	(0.0685)	(0.0425)	(0.0660)
Ongoing mission, regional	0.0871	0.117	0.143
	(0.0751)	(0.0738)	(0.0831)
Mission hosts polity scores	0.0230	−0.239**	−0.169
	(0.0822)	(0.0667)	(0.103)
Mission hosts population (logged)	0.635**	0.170	−0.275
	(0.204)	(0.149)	(0.222)

Table A3 (cont.)

Variable	Token force	Mixed	Non-token force
Mission hosts GDP per capita (logged)	−1.419**	−1.373**	−0.843**
	(0.353)	(0.251)	(0.311)
Constant	−10.84*	−8.979*	−2.635
	(5.398)	(3.623)	(4.884)
Observations	3,621	3,621	3,621
Pseudo R-squared	0.245	0.245	0.245
Chi squared	552.4	552.4	552.4
Log likelihood	−3398	−3398	−3398

Note: Robust standard errors clustered by country in parentheses. ** $p <0.01$, * $p <0.05$

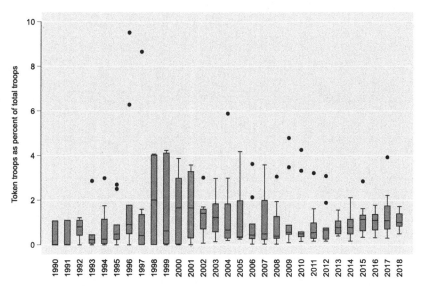

Figure A1 Token troops as percentage of total troops by mission over time

On average, troops from token forces accounted for 1.16% of deployed UN peacekeepers from 1990 to 2018, but there are variations across missions, over time and within each year. Figure A1 presents the box plots of token troops as percentage of total troops for all active missions in a given year from 1990 to 2018. There are a few outliers as represented by the dots. In particular, there are four observations of missions having token forces account for more than 5% of the total deployed troops. These are UNFICYP and UNPROFOR in 1996, UNFICYP in 1997, and UNMISET in 2004. Still, the maximum proportion of token troops is less than 10%, substantially below the 17% average monthly troop shortfall.

References

Acharya, A. (2013). The R2P and norm diffusion: Towards a framework of norm circulation. *Global Responsibility to Protect*, **5**(4), 466–79.

African Union. (2020). *Consultancy Service to Study on Women's Participation in African Union (AU) Peace Operations*. https://au.int/en/bids/20201009/consultancy-service-study-womens-participation-african-union-au-peace-operations.

Andersson, A. (2000). Democracies and UN peacekeeping operations, 1990–1996. *International Peacekeeping*, **7**(2), 1–22.

Bellamy, A. J., & Williams, P. D. (2009). The West and contemporary peace operations. *Journal of Peace Research*, **46**(1), 39–57.

Bellamy, A. J., & Williams, P. D. (2012). *Broadening the Base of United Nations Troop-and Police-Contributing Countries*. Providing for Peacekeeping No. 1. New York: International Peace Institute. www.ipinst.org/wp-content/uploads/publications/ipi_pub_broadening_the_base.pdf.

Bensahel, N. (2007). International alliances and military effectiveness: Fighting alongside allies and partners. In R. A. Brooks & E. A. Stanley, eds., *Creating Military Power: The Sources of Military Effectiveness*. Redwood City, CA: Stanford University Press, pp. 186–206.

Boutellis, A. (2020). Rethinking UN peacekeeping burden-sharing in a time of global disorder. *Fudan Journal of the Humanities and Social Sciences*, **13**(2), 193–209.

Boutellis, A., & Beary, M. (2020). *Sharing the Burden: Lessons from the European Return to Multidimensional Peacekeeping*. New York: International Peace Institute. www.ipinst.org/wp-content/uploads/2020/01/European-Canadian_Final.pdf.

Boutton, A., & D'Orazio, V. (2020). Buying blue helmets: The role of foreign aid in the construction of UN peacekeeping missions. *Journal of Peace Research*, **57**(2), 312–28.

Bove, V., & Elia, L. (2011). Supplying peace: Participation in and troop contribution to peacekeeping missions. *Journal of Peace Research*, **48**(6), 699–714.

Bove, V., Ruffa, C., & Ruggeri, A. (2020). *Composing Peace: Mission Composition in UN Peacekeeping*. Oxford: Oxford University Press.

Bradley, M. (2019). Unintended consequences of adjacency claims: The function and dysfunction of analogies between refugee protection and IDP protection in the work of UNHCR. *Global Governance: A Review of Multilateralism and International Organizations*, **25**(4), 620–44.

Brown, D. P., & Ahram, A. I. (2015). Jordan and the United Arab Emirates: Arab partners in Afghanistan. In G. A. Mattox & S. M. Grenier, eds., *Coalition Challenges in Afghanistan: The Politics of Alliance*. Redwood City, CA: Stanford University Press, pp. 201–13.

Busch, M. L., & Reinhardt, E. (2006). Three's a crowd: Third parties and WTO dispute settlement. *World Politics*, **58**(3), 446–77.

Chavez, R. B. (2015). El Salvador: Exporting security in the national interest. In G. A. Mattox & S. M. Grenier, eds., *Coalition Challenges in Afghanistan: The Politics of Alliance*. Redwood City, CA: Stanford University Press, pp. 80–8.

Coleman, K. P. (2007). *International Organisations and Peace Enforcement*. Cambridge: Cambridge University Press.

Coleman, K. P. (2013). Token troop contributions to United Nations peacekeeping operations. In A. J. Bellamy & P. D. Williams, eds., *Providing Peacekeepers: The Politics, Challenges, and Future of United Nations Peacekeeping Contributions*. Oxford: Oxford University Press, pp. 47–68.

Coleman, K. P. (2017). The legitimacy audience shapes the coalition: Lessons from Afghanistan, 2001. *Journal of Intervention and Statebuilding*, **11**(3), 339–58.

Coleman, K. P. (2020a). Downsizing in UN peacekeeping: The impact on civilian peacekeepers and the missions employing them. *International Peacekeeping*, **27**(5), 703–31.

Coleman, K. P. (2020b). United Nations peacekeeping decisions: Three hierarchies, upward mobility and institutionalised inequality among member states. *Global Society*, **34**(3), 318–34.

Coleman, K. P., & Job, B. L. (2021). Still globalized: How China and Africa may shape UN peacekeeping. *International Affairs*, **97**(5), 1451–68.

Coleman, K. P., Lundgren, M., & Oksamytna, K. (2021). Slow progress on UN rapid deployment: The pitfalls of policy paradigms in international organizations. *International Studies Review*, **23**(3), 455–83.

Coleman, K. P., & Nyblade, B. (2018). Peacekeeping for profit? The scope and limits of "mercenary" UN peacekeeping. *Journal of Peace Research*, **55**(6), 726–41.

Coleman, K. P., & Williams, P. D. (2021). Peace operations are what states make of them: Why future evolution is more likely than extinction. *Contemporary Security Policy*, **42**(2), 241–55.

Cook, M. L. (2000). "Immaculate war": Constraints on humanitarian intervention. *Ethics & International Affairs*, **14**, 55–65.

Cortell, A. P., & Peterson, S. (2001). Limiting the unintended consequences of institutional change. *Comparative Political Studies*, **34**(7), 768–99.

Cunliffe, P. (2013). *Legions of Peace: UN Peacekeepers from the Global South.* London: Hurst.

Daniel, D. C. F. (2013). Contemporary patterns in peace operations, 2000–2010. In A. J. Bellamy & P. D. Williams, eds., *Providing Peacekeepers: The Politics, Challenges, and Future of United Nations Peacekeeping Contributions.* Oxford: Oxford University Press, pp. 25–46.

Daniel, D. C. F., Williams, P. D., & Smith, A. C. (2015). *Deploying Combined Teams: Lessons Learned from Operational Partnerships in UN Peacekeeping.* Providing for Peacekeeping No. 12. New York: International Peace Institute. www.ipinst.org/wp-content/uploads/2015/08/IPI-E-pub-Operational-Partnerships-in-Peacekeeping.pdf.

De Andrade, J. B. (2001, June). Brazilian soldiers in ARGCON. *Blue Beret – THE UNFICYP Magazine.* https://unficyp.unmissions.org/sites/default/files/bb_06_june_2001.pdf.

Di Salvatore, J., Lundgren, M., Oksamytna, K., & Smidt, H. M. (2022). Introducing the peacekeeping mandates (PEMA) dataset. *Journal of Conflict Resolution*, **66**(4–5), 924–51.

Duursma, A., & Gledhill, J. (2019). Voted out: Regime type, elections and contributions to United Nations peacekeeping operations. *European Journal of International Relations*, **25**(4), 1157–85.

Elkins, Z., Guzman, A. T., & Simmons, B. A. (2006). Competing for capital: The diffusion of bilateral investment treaties, 1960–2000. *International Organization*, **60**(4), 811–46.

Fang, S., Li, X., & Sun, F. (2018). China's evolving motivations and goals in UN peacekeeping participation. *International Journal*, **73**(3), 464–73.

Feenstra, R. C., Inklaar, R., & Timmer, M. P. (2015). The next generation of the Penn World Table. *American Economic Review*, **105**(10), 3150–82.

Finnemore, M. (2003). *The Purpose of Intervention: Changing Beliefs about the Use of Force.* Ithaca, NY: Cornell University Press.

Finnemore, M. (2005). Fights about rules: The role of efficacy and power in changing multilateralism. *Review of International Studies*, **31**(S1), 187–206.

Gaibulloev, K., George, J., Sandler, T., & Shimizu, H. (2015). Personnel contributions to UN and non-UN peacekeeping missions: A public goods approach. *Journal of Peace Research*, **52**(6), 727–42.

Gaibulloev, K., Sandler, T., & Shimizu, H. (2009). Demands for UN and non-UN peacekeeping: Nonvoluntary versus voluntary contributions to a public good. *Journal of Conflict Resolution*, **53**(6), 827–52.

Gartner, S. S. (2008). The multiple effects of casualties on public support for war: An experimental approach. *American Political Science Review*, **102**(1), 95–106.

Gelpi, C., Feaver, P. D., & Reifler, J. (2009). *Paying the Human Costs of War.* Princeton, NJ: Princeton University Press.

Gilardi, F. (2012). Transnational diffusion: Norms, ideas, and policies. In W. Carlsnaes, T. Risse, & B. A. Simmons, eds., *Handbook of International Relations*, 2nd ed. Thousand Oaks, CA: Sage, pp. 453–77.

Gilardi, F., Füglister, K., & Luyet, S. (2009). Learning from others: The diffusion of hospital financing reforms in OECD countries. *Comparative Political Studies*, **42**(4), 549–73.

Gjevori, E., & Visoka, G. (2018). Albanian contribution to international peacekeeping: Identity, interests and peacekeeping. *POLIS International Scientific Journal*, **17**, 122–44.

Glasius, M., Schalk, J., & De Lange, M. (2020). Illiberal norm diffusion: How do governments learn to restrict nongovernmental organizations? *International Studies Quarterly*, **64**(2), 453–68.

Graham, E. R., & Serdaru, A. (2020). Power, control, and the logic of substitution in institutional design: The case of international climate finance. *International Organization*, **74**(4), 671–706.

Greenhill, B. (2010). The company you keep: International socialization and the diffusion of human rights norms. *International Studies Quarterly*, **54**(1), 127–45.

Haass, F., & Ansorg, N. (2018). Better peacekeepers, better protection? Troop quality of United Nations peace operations and violence against civilians. *Journal of Peace Research*, **55**(6), 742–58.

Hall, P. A., & Taylor, R. C. (1996). Political science and the three new institutionalisms. *Political Studies*, **44**(5), 936–57.

Hannum, J., & Das, C. (2021, February 25). Presentation at *Overcoming the Money Crisis? The Financing of UN Peacekeeping and the Biden Administration* [digital roundtable]. Leiden University, The Netherlands.

Hay, C., & Wincott, D. (1998). Structure, agency and historical institutionalism. *Political Studies*, **46**(5), 951–7.

Henke, M. E. (2019). *Constructing Allied Cooperation*. Ithaca, NY: Cornell University Press.

High-Level Independent Panel on Peace Operations (HIPPO). (2015). *Report of the High-Level Independent Panel on Peace Operations on Uniting Our Strengths for Peace: Politics, Partnership, and People.* New York: United Nations. www.un.org/en/ga/search/view_doc.asp?symbol=S/2015/446.

Hultman, L., Kathman, J., & Shannon, M. (2013). United Nations peacekeeping and civilian protection in civil war. *American Journal of Political Science*, **57**(4), 875–91.

Hunt, C. T. (2017). All necessary means to what ends? The unintended consequences of the "robust turn" in UN peace operations. *International Peacekeeping*, **24**(1), 108–31.

Hurd, I. (2017). *How to Do Things with International Law*. Princeton, NJ: Princeton University Press.

Hurrell, A. (2005). Legitimacy and the use of force: Can the circle be squared? *Review of International Studies*, **31**(S1), 15–32.

Hynek, N., & Marton, P. (eds.). (2012). *Statebuilding in Afghanistan: Multinational Contributions to Reconstruction*. London: Routledge.

Jakobsen, P. V. (1996). National interest, humanitarianism or CNN: What triggers UN peace enforcement after the Cold War? *Journal of Peace Research*, **33**(2), 205–15.

Jennings, K. M. (2010). Unintended consequences of intimacy: Political economies of peacekeeping and sex tourism. *International Peacekeeping*, **17**(2), 229–43.

Johns, L., & Pelc, K. (2018). Free-riding on enforcement in the WTO. *Journal of Politics*, **80**(3), 873–89.

Johns, R., & Davies, G. A. (2014). Coalitions of the willing? International backing and British public support for military action. *Journal of Peace Research*, **51**(6), 767–81.

Karlsrud, J. (2015). The UN at war: Examining the consequences of peace-enforcement mandates for the UN peacekeeping operations in the CAR, the DRC and Mali. *Third World Quarterly*, **36**(1), 40–54.

Karlsrud, J. (2018). *The UN at War: Peace Operations in a New Era*. Cham, Switzerland: Springer International.

Kathman, J. D. (2013). United Nations peacekeeping personnel commitments, 1990–2011. *Conflict Management and Peace Science*, **30**(5), 532–49.

Kathman, J. D., & Melin, M. M. (2017). Who keeps the peace? Understanding state contributions to UN peacekeeping operations. *International Studies Quarterly*, **61**(1), 150–62.

Kenkel, K. M., de Souza Neto, D. M., & Ribeiro, M. M. L. A. (2020). Peace operations, intervention and Brazilian foreign policy: Key issues and debates. In P. Esteves, M. Gabrielsen, & B. de Carvalho, eds., *Status and the Rise of Brazil*. Cham, Switzerland: Palgrave Macmillan, pp. 133–51.

Koops, J. A., & Tercovich, G. (2016). A European return to United Nations peacekeeping? Opportunities, challenges and ways ahead. *International Peacekeeping*, **23**(5), 597–609.

Kreps, S. E. (2011). *Coalitions of Convenience: United States Military Interventions after the Cold War*. Oxford: Oxford University Press.

Kucik, J., & Peritz, L. (2021). How do third parties affect compliance in the trade regime? *The Journal of Politics*, **83**(3), 1184–9.

Lebovic, J. H. (2004). Uniting for peace? Democracies and United Nations peace operations after the Cold War. *Journal of Conflict Resolution*, **48**(6), 910–36.

Li, X. (2012). Understanding China's behavioral change in the WTO dispute settlement system. *Asian Survey*, **52**(6), 1111–37.

Lundgren, M., Oksamytna, K., & Coleman, K. P. (2021). Only as fast as its troop contributors: Incentives, capabilities, and constraints in the UN's peacekeeping response. *Journal of Peace Research*, **58**(4), 671–86.

March, J. G., & Olsen, J. P. (1983). The new institutionalism: Organizational factors in political life. *American Political Science Review*, **78**(3), 734–49.

Marshall, M. G., & Gurr, T. R. (2014). *Polity IV Project: Political Regime Characteristics and Transitions*. Center for Systemic Peace. www.system icpeace.org/polity/polity4.htm.

Mattox, G. A., & Grenier, S. M. (eds.). (2015). *Coalition Challenges in Afghanistan: The Politics of Alliance*. Redwood City, CA: Stanford University Press.

McDermott, R. (2001). The psychological ideas of Amos Tversky and their relevance for political science. *Journal of Theoretical Politics*, **13**(1), 5–33.

Merton, R. K. (1936). The unanticipated consequences of purposive social action. *American Sociological Review*, **1**(6), 894–904.

Meseguer, C. (2009). *Learning, Policy Making, and Market Reforms*. Cambridge: Cambridge University Press.

Mitchell, J. L., & Petray, E. (2016). The march toward marriage equality: Reexamining the diffusion of same-sex marriage among states. *Public Policy and Administration*, **31**(4), 283–302.

Morey, D. S. (2016). Military coalitions and the outcome of interstate wars. *Foreign Policy Analysis*, **12**(4), 533–51.

Mueller, J. (2004). *The Remnants of War*. Ithaca, NY: Cornell University Press.

Olson, M., & Zeckhauser, R. (1966). An economic theory of alliances. *The Review of Economics and Statistics*, **48**(3), 266–79.

Olsson, L., Schjølset, A., & Möller, F. (2015). Women's participation in international operations and missions. In L. Olsson & T. I. Gizelis, eds., *Gender, Peace and Security*. London: Routledge, pp. 37–61.

Passmore, T. J., Shannon, M., & Hart, A. F. (2018). Rallying the troops: Collective action and self-interest in UN peacekeeping contributions. *Journal of Peace Research*, **55**(3), 366–79.

Paul, C. (2008). US presidential war powers: Legacy chains in military intervention decisionmaking. *Journal of Peace Research*, **45**(5), 665–79.

Pelc, K. (2017). Twenty years of third party participation at the WTO: What have we learned? In M. Elsig, B. Hoekman, & J. Pauwelyn, eds., *Assessing the World Trade Organization: Fit for Purpose?* Cambridge: Cambridge University Press, pp. 203–22.

Perkins, R., & Neumayer, E. (2008). Extra-territorial interventions in conflict spaces: Explaining the geographies of post-cold war peacekeeping. *Political Geography*, **27**(8), 895–914.

Perry, C., & Smith, A. C. (2013). *Trends in Uniformed Contributions to UN Peacekeeping: A New Dataset, 1991–2012*. New York: International Peace Institute. https://papers.ssrn.com/sol3/papers.cfm?abstract_id=2358162.

Pierre, A. J. (2002). *Coalitions Building and Maintenance: The Gulf War, Kosovo, Afghanistan, and the War on Terrorism*. Washington, DC: Georgetown University Institute for the Study of Diplomacy.

Pierson, P., & Skocpol, T. (2002). Historical institutionalism in contemporary political science. In I. Katznelson & H. V. Milner, eds., *Political Science: The State of the Discipline*. New York: W. W. Norton, pp. 693–721.

Pouliot, V. (2016). *International Pecking Orders: The Politics and Practice of Multilateral Diplomacy*. Cambridge: Cambridge University Press.

Raes, S., Du Bois, C., & Buts, C. (2019). Supplying UN peacekeepers: An assessment of the body bag syndrome among OECD nations. *International Peacekeeping*, **26**(1), 111–36.

Rahbek-Clemmensen, J. (2019). The strategic purpose of individual augmentee officers for junior partners in multinational military operations. *Defense & Security Analysis*, **35**(4), 343–61.

Raitasalo, J. (2014). Moving beyond the "Western expeditionary frenzy." *Comparative Strategy*, **33**(4), 372–88.

Recchia, S. (2015). *Reassuring the Reluctant Warriors: US Civil-Military Relations and Multilateral Intervention*. Ithaca, NY: Cornell University Press.

Schmitt, O. (2019). More allies, weaker missions? How junior partners contribute to multinational military operations. *Contemporary Security Policy*, **40**(1), 70–84. https://doi.org/10.1080/13523260.2018.1501999.

Shanker, T. (2011, June 10). Defense Secretary warns NATO of "dim" future. *The New York Times*. www.nytimes.com/2011/06/11/world/europe/11gates.html.

Simmons, B. A., Dobbin, F., & Garrett, G. (2006). Introduction: The international diffusion of liberalism. *International Organization*, **60**(4), 781–810.

Smith, A. C., & Boutellis, A. (2013). *Rethinking Force Generation: Filling the Capability Gaps in UN Peacekeeping*. Providing for Peacekeeping No. 2. New York: International Peace Institute. https://ciaotest.cc.columbia.edu/wps/ipi/0028443/f_0028443_23122.pdf.

Snyder, G. H. (1997). *Alliance Politics*. Ithaca, NY: Cornell University Press.

Snyder, J. (2020). Backlash against human rights shaming: Emotions in groups. *International Theory*, **12**(1), 109–32. https://doi.org/10.1017/S175297191 9000216.

Solar, C. (2019). Chile's peacekeeping and the post-UN intervention scenario in Haiti. *International Studies*, **56**(4), 272–91.

Stinnett, D. M., Tir, J., Diehl, P. F., Schafer, P., & Gochman, C. (2002). The correlates of war (COW) project direct contiguity data, version 3.0. *Conflict Management and Peace Science*, **19**(2), 59–67.

SWI swissinfo.ch. (2007, November 21). *Swiss Pull Military Staff Out of Afghanistan*. www.swissinfo.ch/eng/swiss-pull-military-staff-out-of-afghani stan/6269320.

Thelen, K. (1999). Historical institutionalism in comparative politics. *Annual Review of Political Science*, **2**(1), 369–404.

Thelen, K. (2004). *How Institutions Evolve: The Political Economy of Skills in Germany, Britain, the United States, and Japan*. Cambridge: Cambridge University Press.

Thompson, A. (2006). Coercion through IOs: The Security Council and the logic of information transmission. *International Organization*, **60**(1), 1–34.

Ulrich, M. P. (2015). The Visegrad Four: Achieving long-term security through alliance support. In G. A. Mattox & S. M. Grenier, eds., *Coalition Challenges in Afghanistan: The Politics of Alliance*. Redwood City, CA: Stanford University Press, pp. 157–69.

UN. (1960, September 21). *First Progress Report to the Secretary-General from His Special Representative in the Congo, Ambassador Rajeshwar Daval*. UN Document S/4531. https://documents-dds-ny.un.org/doc/UNDOC/GEN/N60/228/94/pdf/N6022894.pdf?OpenElement.

UN. (2002). *Selection Standards and Training Guidelines for United Nations Military Observers*. UN Department of Peacekeeping Operations. http://christusliberat.org/wp-content/uploads/2017/10/ENG_UN_Guide-for-mili tary-observers.pdf.

UN. (2017a). *Report of the Special Committee on Peacekeeping Operations, 2017 Substantive Session (New York, 21 February–17 March 2017)*. UN General Assembly. https://digitallibrary.un.org/record/1290750?ln=en.

UN. (2017b, June 30). *Summary of Contributions to UN Peacekeeping by Country, Mission and Post: Police, UN Military Experts on Mission, Staff Officers and Troops*. https://peacekeeping.un.org/sites/default/files/jun17_3.pdf.

UN. (2019). *Uniformed Gender Parity Strategy 2018–2028*. UN Department of Peace Operations. https://peacekeeping.un.org/sites/default/files/uniformed-gender-parity-2018-2028.pdf.

UN. (2020a). *The Protection of Civilians in United Nations Peacekeeping Handbook*. UN Department of Peace Operations. https://peacekeeping.un .org/sites/default/files/dpo_poc_handbook_final_as_printed.pdf.

UN. (2020b, December 31). *Summary of Contribution to UN Peacekeeping by Country, Mission and Post. Police, UN Military Experts on Mission, Staff Officers, and Troops*. https://peacekeeping.un.org/sites/default/files/03_country_ and_mission_33_dec2020.pdf.

UN. (2020c, January). *Uniformed Capability Requirements: MINUSMA Special Edition*. UN Department of Peace Operations. https://pcrs.un.org/Lists/ Resources/03-%20Uniformed%20Capability%20Requirements%20for% 20UN%20Peacekeeping/2020/MINUSMA%20Force%20Adaptation% 20Plan%20Uniformed%20Capability%20Requirements_Jan%202020.pdf.

UN. (2021a, April 30). *Contribution of Uniformed Personnel to UN by Country and Personnel Type: Experts on Mission, Formed Police Units, Individual Police, Staff Officer, and Troops*. https://peacekeeping.un.org/sites/default/ files/01-summary_of_contributions_37_apr2021.pdf.

UN. (2021b, July 31). *Contribution of Uniformed Personnel to UN by Country and Personnel Type: Experts on Mission, Formed Police Units, Individual Police, Staff Officer, and Troops*. https://peacekeeping.un.org/sites/default/ files/01_summary_of_contribution_40_july2021.pdf.

UN. (2021c, March). *Current and Emerging Uniformed Capability Requirements for United Nations Peacekeeping*. https://pcrs.un.org/Lists/ Resources/03-%20Uniformed%20Capability%20Requirements%20for% 20UN%20Peacekeeping/2021/Uniformed%20Capability%20Requirements %20for%20UN%20Peacekeeping_March%2021_final.pdf.

UN. (2021d). *Historical Uniformed Personnel Contribution Dataset*. https:// psdata.un.org/dataset/DPO-UCHISTORICAL

UN. (2021e, July 31). *Monthly Summary of Military and Police Contributions to United Nations Operations*. https://peacekeeping.un.org/sites/default/ files/00-front_page_msr_july_2021.pdf.

UN. (2021f, January 31). *Summary of Military and Police Personnel by Mission and Posts: Police, UN Military Experts on Mission, Staff Officers and Troop*. https://peacekeeping.un.org/sites/default/files/06_mission_and_post_34_ jan2021.pdf.

UN. (2021g, February 28). *Uniformed Personnel Contributing Countries by Ranking: Experts on Mission, Formed Police Units, Individual Police, Staff Officer, and Troops*. https://peacekeeping.un.org/sites/default/files/02-country_ ranking_35_feb2021.pdf.

UN. (2021h, May). *United Nations Manual for the Generation and Deployment of Military and Formed Police Units to Peace Operations*. https://pcrs.un

.org/Lists/Resources/04-%20Force%20and%20Police%20Generation%20Process/Force%20Generation%20Documents%20(Military)/2021.05%20Manual%20for%20Generation%20and%20Deployment%20of%20MIL%20and%20FPU.pdf.

UN Department of Peacekeeping Operations, & UN Department of Field Support (UNDPKO & UNDFS). (2009, July). *A New Partnership Agenda: Charting a New Horizon for UN Peacekeeping.* https://peacekeeping.un.org/sites/default/files/newhorizon_0.pdf.

UN Department of Peacekeeping Operations, & UN Department of Field Support (UNDPKO & UNDFS). (2012, August). *United Nations Infantry Battalion Manual*, Volume 2. https://peacekeeping.un.org/sites/default/files/peacekeeping/en/UNIBAM.Vol.II.pdf.

UN. (2016, January 31). UN Missions Summary of Military and Police. https://peacekeeping.un.org/sites/default/files/jan16_6.pdf

UN Department of Peacekeeping Operations & UN Department of Field Support (UNDPKO & UNDFS). (2017, March). *Guidelines: United Nations Military Overserves (UNMO) in Peacekeeping Operations.* Ref. 2016.25. https://pcrs.un.org/Lists/Resources/04-%20Force%20and%20Police%20Generation%20Process/Force%20Generation%20Documents%20(Military)/2016.25%20Guidelines%20on%20UN%20Military%20Observers%20in%20Peacekeeping%20Operations.pdf.

UN Development Programme. (n.d.). *Elsie Initiative Fund for Uniformed Women in Peace Operations.* Multi-Partner Trust Fund Office. http://mptf.undp.org/factsheet/fund/EIF00.

UN Peacekeeping Force in Cyprus (UNFICYP). (2019). *Blue Beret Spring/Summer 2019.* https://unficyp.unmissions.org/sites/default/files/bb-_summer_2019-_special_edition_-_web.pdf.

UN Peacekeeping Force in Cyprus (UNFICYP). (2021). *Young Peacekeepers* [podcast]. https://soundcloud.com/user-323635215/podcast-april-young-peacekeepers.

UN Secretary-General. (1956, November 6). *Second and Final Report of the Secretary-General on the Plan for an Emergency International United Nations Force Requested in the Resolution Adopted by the General Assembly on 4 November 1956.* UN Document A/3302. UN General Assembly. https://documents-dds-ny.un.org/doc/UNDOC/GEN/N56/296/23/PDF/N5629623.pdf?OpenElement.

UN Secretary-General. (1964, September 10). *Report by the Secretary-General on the United Nations Operation in Cyprus.* UN Document S/5950. UN Security Council. www.securitycouncilreport.org/atf/cf/%7B65BFCF9B-6D27-4E9C-8CD3-CF6E4FF96FF9%7D/Cyprus%20S%205950.pdf.

UN Secretary-General. (1975, May 21). *Report of the Secretary-General on the UN Disengagement Observer Force, for the Period 27 November 1974–21 May 1975*. UN Document S/11694. UN Security Council. https://digitalli brary.un.org/record/457434/?ln=fr.

UN Secretary-General. (1979, June 8). *Report of the Secretary-General on the United Nations Interim Force in Lebanon (for the Period from 13 January to 8 June 1979)*. UN Document S/13384. UN Security Council. https://digitalli brary.un.org/record/2931?ln=en.

UN Secretary-General. (1999, June 8). *Report of the Secretary-General on the United Nations Operation in Cyprus (for the Period from 9 December 1998 to 9 June 1999)*. UN Document S/1999/657. UN Security Council. www .cyprusun.org/?p=2865.

UN Secretary-General. (2021, February 19). *Report of the Secretary-General on Budget for the United Nations Multidimensional Integrated Stabilization Mission in Mali (for the Period from 1 July 2021 to 30 June 2022)*. UN Document A/75/767. UN General Assembly. https:// undocs.org/A/75/767.

UN Secretary-General. (2020b, November 3). *Report of the Secretary-General on Implementation of the Recommendations of the Special Committee on Peacekeeping Operations*. UN Document A/75/763. UN General Assembly. https://digitallibrary.un.org/record/3894243?ln=en.

UN Security Council (UNSC). (2020, August 28). *Resolution 2538 (2020)*. https://undocs.org/en/S/RES/2538(2020).

United States Joint Chiefs of Staff. (2007, March 7). *Joint Publication 3–16: Multinational Operations*. www.bits.de/NRANEU/others/jp-doctrine/jp3_ 16%2807%29.pdf.

Victor, J. (2010). African peacekeeping in Africa: Warlord politics, defense economics, and state legitimacy. *Journal of Peace Research*, **47**(2), 217–29.

Voeten, E. (2005). The political origins of the UN Security Council's ability to legitimize the use of force. *International Organization*, **59**(3), 527–57.

Von Billerbeck, S., & Tansey, O. (2019). Enabling autocracy? Peacebuilding and post-conflict authoritarianism in the Democratic Republic of Congo. *European Journal of International Relations*, **25**(3), 698–722.

Wainhouse, D. (1973). *International Peacekeeping at the Crossroads: National Support–Experience and Prospects*. Baltimore, MD: Johns Hopkins University Press.

Walt, S. M. (1987). *The Origins of Alliances*. Ithaca, NY: Cornell University Press.

Waltz, K. N. (1979). *Theory of International Politics*. Reading, MA: Addison-Wesley.

Ward, H., & Dorussen, H. (2016). Standing alongside your friends: Network centrality and providing troops to UN peacekeeping operations. *Journal of Peace Research*, **53**(3), 392–408.

Weeks, G. (2017). Fighting to close the School of the Americas: Unintended consequences of successful activism. *Journal of Human Rights*, **16**(2), 178–92.

Weitsman, P. A. (2013). *Waging War: Alliances, Coalitions, and Institutions of Interstate Violence*. Redwood City, CA: Stanford University Press.

Western, J. (2002). Sources of humanitarian intervention: Beliefs, information, and advocacy in the US decisions on Somalia and Bosnia. *International Security*, **26**(4), 112–42.

Weyland, K. (2012). The Arab Spring: Why the surprising similarities with the revolutionary wave of 1848? *Perspectives on Politics*, **10**(4), 917–34.

Wheeler, N. J. (2000). *Saving Strangers: Humanitarian Intervention in International Society*. Oxford: Oxford University Press.

Williams, P. D. (2020). The Security Council's peacekeeping trilemma. *International Affairs*, **96**(2), 479–99.

Wolford, S. (2015). *The Politics of Military Coalitions*. Cambridge: Cambridge University Press.

World Bank. (2021). *World Development Indicators*. Washington, DC: The World Bank.

World Trade Organization (WTO). (2020). *Understanding the WTO: Settling Disputes*. www.wto.org/english/thewto_e/whatis_e/tif_e/disp1_e.htm.

Young, G. (2019). Political decision-making and the decline of Canadian peacekeeping. *Canadian Foreign Policy Journal*, **25**(2), 152–71.

Zhukov, Y. M., & Stewart, B. M. (2013). Choosing your neighbors: Networks of diffusion in international relations. *International Studies Quarterly*, **57**(2), 271–87.

Ziai, F. (2009). Broadening the base of contributors to United Nations peacekeeping: Proposals for how the United Nations can attract and support new, expanding and returning troop- and police-contributing countries. In *Challenges Forum Report 2009*. Stockholm: International Forum for the Challenges of Peace Operations, pp. 29–52.

Acknowledgments

This research was supported by the Social Sciences and Humanities Research Council of Canada (F18-01522). Many thanks to all the individuals who consented to be interviewed for this project, generously taking the time to share their insights and expertise. Over the course of this project, James Anderson, Alex Bland, Lindsey Cox, Nicolas Dragojlovic, Saleh Ismail, Tricia Lo, Josh Medicoff, Paul Narvestad, and Sule Yaylaci contributed valuable research assistance. Parker Li and Dania Sheldon contributed editorial assistance toward the preparation of the final manuscript. We are grateful to all our colleagues who provided comments on different iterations of the research, including discussants and audience members at meetings of the International Studies Association and the American Political Science Association. We particularly thank Richard Caplan, Marina Henke, Brian Job, Angel O'Mahony, Richard Price, Sarah von Billerbeck, Paul Williams, and Ngaire Woods for their insights and support of the project. We also gratefully acknowledge our anonymous reviewer's insightful and constructive comments and the expert guidance Jon Pevehouse and Sarah Kreps provided.

Cambridge Elements ☰

International Relations

Series Editors

Jon C. W. Pevehouse
University of Wisconsin–Madison

Jon C. W. Pevehouse is the Vilas Distinguished Achievement Professor of Political Science at the University of Wisconsin–Madison. He has published numerous books and articles in IR in the fields of international political economy, international organizations, foreign policy analysis, and political methodology. He is a former editor of the leading IR field journal, International Organization.

Tanja A. Börzel
Freie Universität Berlin

Tanja A. Börzel is the Professor of political science and holds the Chair for European Integration at the Otto-Suhr-Institute for Political Science, Freie Universität Berlin. She holds a PhD from the European University Institute, Florence, Italy. She is coordinator of the Research College "The Transformative Power of Europe," as well as the FP7-Collaborative Project "Maximizing the Enlargement Capacity of the European Union" and the H2020 Collaborative Project "The EU and Eastern Partnership Countries: An Inside-Out Analysis and Strategic Assessment." She directs the Jean Monnet Center of Excellence "Europe and its Citizens."

Edward D. Mansfield
University of Pennsylvania

Edward D. Mansfield is the Hum Rosen Professor of Political Science, University of Pennsylvania. He has published well over 100 books and articles in the area of international political economy, international security, and international organizations. He is Director of the Christopher H. Browne Center for International Politics at the University of Pennsylvania and former program co-chair of the American Political Science Association.

Editorial Team

International Relations Theory
Jeffrey T. Checkel, European
University Institute, Florence
Miles Kahler, American University
Washington, D.C.

International Political Economy
Edward D. Mansfield, University of
Pennsylvania
Stafanie Walter, University of Zurich

International Security
Sarah Kreps, Cornell University
Anna Leander, Graduate Institute
Geneva

International Organisations
Tanja A. Börzel, Freie Universität
Berlin
Jon C. W. Pevehouse, University of
Wisconsin–Madison

Cambridge Elements $\equiv$

International Relations

Elements in the Series

Weak States at Global Climate Negotiations
Federica Genovese

Social Media and International Relations
Sarah Kreps

*Across Type, Time and Space: American Grand Strategy in
Comparative Perspective*
Peter Dombrowski and Simon Reich

Moral Psychology, Neuroscience, and International Norms
Richard Price and Kathryn Sikkink

Contestations of the Liberal International Order
Fredrik Söderbaum, Kilian Spandler, Agnese Pacciardi

Domestic Interests, Democracy, and Foreign Policy Change
Brett Ashley Leeds, Michaela Mattes

*Token Forces: How Tiny Troop Deployments Became Ubiquitous in UN
Peacekeeping*
Katharina P. Coleman, Xiaojun Li

A full series listing is available at: www.cambridge.org/EIR

Printed in the United States
by Baker & Taylor Publisher Services